How Honesty Pays

How Honesty Pays

Restoring Integrity to the Workplace

Charles E. Watson

Westport, Connecticut
London

Library of Congress Cataloging-in-Publication Data

Watson, Charles E.
 How honesty pays : restoring integrity to the workplace / Charles E. Watson.
  p. cm.
 Includes bibliographical references and index.
 ISBN 0-275-98787-6 (alk. paper)
  1. Business ethics.   2. Integrity.   3. Organizational behavior.
4. Corporate culture.   I. Title.
 HF5387.W378 2005
 174'.4–dc22   2005018686

British Library Cataloguing in Publication Data is available.

Library of Congress Catalog Card Number: 2005018686
ISBN: 0-275-98787-6

First published in 2005

Praeger Publishers, 88 Post Road West, Westport, CT 06881
An imprint of Greenwood Publishing Group, Inc.
www.praeger.com

Printed in the United States of America

The paper used in this book complies with the
Permanent Paper Standard issued by the National
Information Standards Organization (Z39.48-1984).

10 9 8 7 6 5 4 3 2 1

Contents

Preface

You probably would not have picked this book off the shelf if you didn't already believe honesty is important. Of course it is. It pays to be honest—we know that. But there is more to honesty than just its long-term benefits. There is something special about those we know to be honest. They are especially attractive human beings. As if by some magnetic-like force, we are inexplicably drawn to them. We like them. We like being around them. We wish more people were like them. And, secretly, we want to be more like them ourselves. But just like many other people who struggle to get by and move ahead in a challenging and competitive world, we also know that being consistently honest isn't easy.

We all know of some places in our lives where we are not entirely honest with ourselves or others. The truth is we are human. We are imperfect beings. Yet it is also true that as humans we are changeable creatures. We have the freedom and capacity to say, "I'm sorry. I want to do better," and then go out and do something about it. That's where this book comes in. It is written to give the serious reader practical ideas others have used successfully to move themselves along the path to greater levels of honesty and integrity, particularly in the workplace but in other realms of their lives as well.

The more deeply we consider the quality of honesty, the more we are amazed at the hold it has on the human heart. While minds can understand the wisdom behind honest dealings, it is our hearts that are most captivated by honesty. It is no mere accident of nature that a good feeling overwhelms us whenever we hear stories of people acting with honesty, especially when the temptations to behave otherwise are so strong. Our very human reaction to honesty suggests there is something far deeper and far more important in honesty than an abstract ideal that our minds tell us is good and desirable. We, therefore, want to know more about honesty so we can make this amazing quality a main element of ourselves.

This is not a book of theories and abstract models for making difficult ethical choices. We leave those matters for the philosophers to debate among themselves. Instead, we will consider here what can best help the average person who has to face life as it is and struggle to get by in a complex, competitive world. We will uncover what dominates the minds and hearts of those whom we most admire for having integrity. This book reveals what they have found effective in guiding their lives. Readers will be invited to look more deeply at themselves to see how their feelings and desires affect their choices. We take this approach because the beliefs, wants, and drives that a person holds dear on the inside are what determine how that person chooses and acts on the outside. The book's many, simple stories reveal deep and powerful truths that you may choose to incorporate in your life. While we may not always know what the right thing to do is or want to do it, we can still be certain of one thing: we are always better off when we are honest, when we act with integrity. The hopeful message of this book is that, like many other successful people, you, too, can develop the quality of honesty in your life and help restore integrity to the workplace.

Charles E. Watson
Oxford, Ohio

How Honesty Pays

CHAPTER 1

Value Honesty

Know the power of integrity in the workplace

Suppose an intelligent creature from outer space were to arrive on earth with the expressed purpose of observing and reporting on what occurs in our work lives. After seeing and recording all that goes on within view and thoughtfully deducing the nature of events hidden, our visitor would surely have much to tell us. Beyond this alien's descriptions of how goods and services are created, distributed, sold, and used—not to mention all the telephone calls, e-mails, and meetings that occurred in between—many of us would be curious to learn our guest's reactions to those things that daily most hurt, discourage, and drag us down. Likewise we'd be quick to notice whether the space alien were perceptive enough to recognize those forces that evoke our admiration, inspire us to improve, and lift our spirits.

Listen thoughtfully to what's spoken in hallways, on factory floors, and in office cubicles in the workplace and you'll learn much about the nature of humans. Beyond the prosaic and the petty gossip, with juicy bits of news discussed, you will find judgments. It is not an insignificant matter that we become outraged when we hear people lying to get what they want or bad-mouthing others they don't like. It says much about us, when we're revolted by underhanded schemes to get ahead and by shabby treatment of others. It becomes obvious that human creatures have a moral capacity when they sense something is decidedly wrong with creating falsified financial statements, shredding documents to cover up misdeeds, exploiting employees, and taking excessive compensation. The fact that we feel gladdened and inspired by admirable actions—like being honest, fair, open-minded, decent, dependable—ought not to be ignored. Likewise, the fact that our passions become outraged and our hearts saddened by opposite behaviors says something profound about our very nature. Our mental and emotional responses to acts admirable or despicable suggests that our humanity is grounded in our capacity to gauge things as being good or bad, ennobling or corrosive. From this realization, we can safely conclude that our dignity rests on how faithfully we exercise this capacity wisely and choose to be guided by the highest ideals in all we do.

It's worth considering whether our guest from space would have the same level of insight as we have, whether he can see beyond the obvious, as we can, and whether he values the importance of moral issues that concern us daily. On such matters we can only speculate but in doing so we come to a more important issue. It is this: Could another civilization advance scientifically and form effective, complex organizations capable of creating and producing things without reliance on the same truths and principles that we honor? I don't know how to prove it conclusively, but I believe it is not possible for that to happen. I cannot imagine how a civilization could flourish, for its arts and sciences to progress, without reliance on the same core values we know—values that recognize truth and beauty, that honor fairness, and that respect the uniqueness and value of persons. If you doubt this, consider the difficulty science would find itself in if scientists were not honest. If their conclusions were untruthful, it would be impossible for science to advance, for findings and conclusions to be respected and confirmed by other scientists. Clearly, good science demands honesty, and so does every other undertaking and profession. It is inconceivable that NASA could launch a space probe to another planet or send a shuttle on a successful mission if the thousands of people who carry out these ventures were dishonest with each other. And neither could a collection of beings from another planet. If our logic is correct, we are left with an important conclusion: The basic truths and principles that have come down to us through the experiences of countless generations and the revelations given us from sources greater than ourselves are, indeed, universal.

We can only suspect that our imaginary visitor from outer space would likely see the connection that exists between the virtues we know—things like truthfulness, fairness, and self-control—and what uplifts and what degrades humans. We would hope that this visitor would recognize the impact honesty has on the quality of an individual's performance and an organization's success. But none of that really matters as much as what we know our experience tells us. And that is, integrity matters—it matters a great deal.

Workplace Challenges to Acting with Integrity

We are wise, here at the start, to face squarely the very real and troubling difficulties that befuddle our best intentions to live by high ideals. In so many ways, circumstances on the job conspire against people, killing off their creative impulses, making them unwilling to get along with others, wasting their talents, and enticing them to be shallow and small and self-seeking. A quick cataloging of workplace pressures and conditions enables us to realize this is true:

- Its never-ending stream of demands does not permit the time to think, to reflect, to savor the moment, to find places to apply our innate talents, to consider fully how our choices and actions will impact others.

- Its emphasis on competition and productivity makes many of us act in ways we cannot admire, leading us to be less the kind of person we'd prefer to be.

- It asks us to perform work that we don't fully believe in or value, and sometimes this includes doing things that we don't feel fully proud of doing.

- It misleads us into craving things that appear important but that turn out to matter very little and not give us the happiness and lasting satisfaction with ourselves that we thought they would.

- In an atmosphere where there are only a few "winners," we sometimes feel that we have less self-worth than we know to be true. This atmosphere makes us feel that our co-workers are potential enemies, not real friends.

In watching how these forces work against our finest intentions, we notice they follow a pattern. They make their first assaults on the most vulnerable places of the human soul—on our greed, pride, hate, resentment, anger, jealousy. From there they launch larger attacks whenever unwholesome wants swell beyond better judgment and right desires. They advance whenever we retreat from our ideals. And as this occurs, we become less creative, less service-minded, less reliable, less likeable, less able to perform effectively, and less satisfied with who we are. The challenge before each person is this: make yourself into a first-class person and performer by living with integrity every minute of every day.

Integrity

What is integrity? The word "integrity" comes from the Latin *integritas*, meaning "whole" or "oneness." People whose behavior is consistent with what they say they honor have this kind of wholeness. Nowadays integrity is generally regarded to mean living up to the highest ideals society honors—truthfulness, courage, decency, fair play, and so forth.

While driving on a busy street one evening, something came crashing down onto my car. It startled me and I jumped. The thing seemed to fall from the sky, and it landed with a huge "thud" right before my eyes on my windshield. I heard the glass give but it didn't crack. I pulled over, stopped my car, and got out to investigate. At first I thought a tree limb had broken off and fallen down, but none was visible. My eyes scanned the roadside, and I spotted a twisted section of a rusted-out tailpipe lying in the gutter. It is possible that a passing car struck it, flipping it high into the air. It came back down, landing on my car. The object made minor abrasions on my windshield but it didn't break it. The safety glass held up under the pounding, its integrity intact. I think this is much like how we are tested daily by life's stormy blasts and temptations. Our record of holding up under assaults, not cracking or breaking, is a fair gauge of our integrity.

There is no greater reward in life than to be found worthy of the full trust of others. If you are lucky, you probably have known at least one person in whom you had complete confidence. When others might take a less honorable path, this person wouldn't even consider such a thing. And if this person held your checkbook, you wouldn't worry about missing a dime. In plain language, temptation would not budge them from their steadfast commitment to what's right. Indeed, you could trust that person no matter what. We all know people whom we would trust with our lives and all we own. We trust them because of their consistent dependability and truthfulness. They never disappoint us; they never let us down.

There is something more to integrity that is worth mentioning. A person of integrity lives up to high ideals, not because of external force or social pressures but because that person is genuinely committed to those high ideals from vast, internal resources of principled desires. Just think of it. What happens on the outside of this person does not penetrate the steadfastness of purpose and reliable actions that are guided by the qualities within this person. Here is someone who can be counted on, through thick or thin, to always take the high road, regardless of whether anyone is watching. The person with integrity is not one to bend the rules when it is convenient or when temptations are strong—not even "just this once." This is a person who is incorruptible, and you can tell it by things both large and small.

Amos Alonzo Stagg was respected and admired for any number of things. Notably, he produced many winning teams during the 42 years he coached football and baseball at the University of Chicago. He also gave the game of football the huddle, the man in motion, and the end around plays. Coach Stagg was also known for his integrity and uncompromising honesty, qualities he put ahead of winning.

Once, when Stagg's baseball team was defending its college title, a batter singled and one of Chicago's players was racing home with the winning run. Stagg shouted at him, "Get back to third base. You cut it by a yard." "But the umpire didn't see it," the player protested. "That doesn't make any difference," roared Stagg. "Get back!" It cost Chicago the game but a player had won a valuable lesson in character.

The Contagion of Good and Evil

Many leaders have demonstrated in various ways that ethical standards begin at the top. What leaders do affects what their subordinates do. I recall once being in the office of a director of mining operations. He was a fine and cordial man; everyone liked him, including me. During our conversation, he mentioned a problem they had. Employees, he said, were stealing supplies from the company, taking them home for their own use. He thought we should address the problem and I agreed. We had barely finished talking about this topic when his telephone rang. I could hardly believe what I heard next. The director told one of the company's foremen to go to his private residence with a crew of men and finish a small addition to his house.

Always having to "put out fires"—that's what happens when those at the top are not entirely ethical. Whether they realize it, leaders set the moral tone for their organizations. How they behave gets copied by those around them, particularly by those at lower echelons. Many a person will say to himself as he does something that he knows to be wrong, "This won't hurt anyone." This belief is seriously flawed and there are plenty of illustrations in everyday life that prove it. All acts, good or ill, have a way of weaving their effects into the lives of others.

We know that there are some people in whose company we are inclined to be good. There is an aura about them that evokes decency in everyone they encounter. And, too, there are also certain other people in whose company it is easy for standards to be relaxed. They make getting what's wanted by skirting ethical standards sound okay. The danger they present is not so much a matter of their own ill deeds but rather the power of their ill deeds in misleading others into unwanted behaviors. One of the greatest things any person can do for others is set a good example. This is because there are many people in this world who simply do not have the moral strength to take a stand by themselves. If someone gives them a lead, they will follow. The world needs more good examples, stout souls who will rise up and say, "I will not be a party to this." When that happens, first one follower, then another, and another and another will rise to say, "Neither will I."

How Integrity Makes a Difference in Business

Integrity makes a profound difference in all realms of human conduct, but our focus here will be on how it works in the realm of work. Here is an inspiring illustration of how the concept of integrity can be translated into practical application. In a newspaper column a few years back, Hugh Aaron of Belfast, Maine, described what happened when he ran his business with integrity. From his association with his father's upholstering business, Hugh grew up knowing how easy it is for a vendor to cheat a customer. The customer couldn't possibly know until years later the quality of materials hidden beneath the cover of an overstuffed chair. His father lived by a higher standard, always give customers fair value, even though many of his competitors were not.

Knowledge of these practices led Hugh Aaron to become skeptical of the level of honesty in business overall. His concerns served him well when, years later, he became an entrepreneur making color concentrates for the plastics industry. In that business, Hugh knew that he could get away for a while using cheaper pigments or off-grade plastic matrices. But, he didn't. Also, in that business, occasional mistakes and omissions occurred in billings—a supplier would forget to send a bill for materials shipped or a vendor might have billed them too little or not at all. These temptations showed up from time to time. But Hugh was not going to be corrupted. He refused to take the easy path to quick gains and then rationalize his wrongdoing afterward with the frequently heard excuse, "Everyone else is doing it." Rather than take advantage of these situations by remaining silent, Hugh Aaron instructed his staff to inform the parties of their errors, and his employees eagerly did so.

In Hugh's business, there were no under-the-table payments, no free vacations, no nights on the town, no bedroom companions—none of these things. Business was conducted on strictly business terms and it worked quite well. In fact, his business performed far better than it would have had he operated on less stringent standards.

Hugh's highly moral approach to business caused employees to take pride in their organization, because they could take pride in themselves. Policies grounded in simple honesty created a feeling of mutual trust. Many of his employees remarked that they liked working for a "straight" company. Hugh was not a leader who would tell employees he couldn't afford this or that and then go out and buy himself an overpriced luxury car. The rank-and-file employees, those who made his company successful, were compensated fairly. There wasn't greed at the top, and there wasn't a union to protect the folks at the bottom. Other benefits from this moral approach followed. Customers remained loyal and vendors always took care of Hugh's production needs and other requests. His firm became known as a company of integrity. As a consequence, morale rocketed upward, productivity improved, and customers felt they were well served. And sales and profits kept climbing.

An Enduring Quality

Integrity is not a new idea. It's been around for thousands of years, long before the building of the pyramids. And in all that time, its influence has always been distinctly positive, making tremendous improvement in people and all that they do. There are many ways of illustrating the profound impact integrity makes on businesses. And it's worth looking at prize specimens of this enduring quality in action. Here are two illustrations: The first one is about an entrepreneur named Barney who acquired integrity at an early age and never let go of it. Ultimately, it led to his success. Barney loved and obeyed his mother, and her strict standards shaped the direction his life took.

At 13 Barney was forced to quit school and go to work, because his father's business had failed during the panic of 1873. His first job was in a drug store, but that didn't pay enough. So he left home to work as a farm hand. Farm life wasn't easy. The work day began at 4:30 in the morning and ended only after all the animals were fed and bedded in their stalls. But Barney was strong willed and determined. He developed self-discipline and the habit of working hard, long hours.

His next job was that of a peddler back home in Cincinnati, a job that paid better than farm work. But after a couple of years, his earnings began to slip, as making sales became increasingly more difficult. Barney had a keen mind and saw the reason why. Customers felt they weren't receiving full value for their money. Barney's employer was cutting corners, buying cheaper goods and charging full price. In his later years Barney recalled, "This was my first experience with the principle that you can't fool people." He quit that job and moved on to another—selling tea and coffee for William White and Company, where he drove a delivery wagon and took orders three days a week. The other days he worked behind the counter.

But business faltered for this company too, and again young Barney spotted the reason. It was poor customer service. The owners of William White and Company were incompetent; they lost nearly all their initial investment and young Barney made mental notes as to why. Desperate, the owners offered Barney the job of managing their firm. He accepted on the condition that he'd have the final say in business decisions and receive 10 percent of the profits. They agreed.

As a manager, Barney changed things around. He first moved to improve customer service. He discharged incompetent employees and retained good ones. He kept his delivery boy and hired a cashier to wait on customers and keep an eye on the cash. Barney ordered a new cash register from NCR in nearby Dayton to discourage the owners from "dipping into the till." Barney demanded hard work but he always worked even harder himself. As an early riser, Barney had no difficulty starting the workday before dawn. In the summer months he opened the store at 5 o'clock in the morning—while competitors slept. By the time his competitors had opened their stores, Barney had already taken in half his day's receipts. His trick was a simple one. He put his customers' interests ahead of his own convenience. He knew that the produce farmers who supplied his store came to town very early to deliver their fresh fruits and vegetables. Barney wasn't about to keep them waiting. Because his store opened first, he got the pick of the best produce and he earned the favor of farmers, too.

Barney was determined to give his customers what they paid for—quality products. Customers recognized this and it paid off. His business thrived. Sales increased. By the end of the first year, profits were up and the balance sheet looked good. Barney felt that by rescuing the business from certain failure, he ought to become a full-fledged partner. He offered to buy one third of the business. The two partners laughed at him. Barney quit. He'd begin his own business.

But Barney's savings were insufficient to launch an enterprise on his own. So he turned to a friend. Together they had enough to get started. Barney was only 23 years old when he and his partner, B. A. Branagan, opened their little store on July 1, 1883, in downtown Cincinnati. It was called the Great Western Tea Company. Their first year was not an easy one. Tragedies struck. Each one was a body blow to their tiny enterprise. Through carelessness, Branagan attempted to beat out a train at a crossing. It was a dumb thing to do. The collision destroyed their delivery wagon and killed the horse. The next setback was a flood. The mighty Ohio overflowed its banks. Three feet of water covered their store, destroying their entire stock. But Barney's positive attitude wasn't dampened a bit; he resolved to try even harder.

Another year passed and the small firm was once again in the black and profits were rising. Barney stuck to the principle of fair dealings. He priced his goods low, making a small profit margin on each transaction. But he more than made up for it with higher turnover. Customers got full value for their money and his business prospered with greater overall profit.

A dapper, fast-talking salesman called on Barney once, trying to sell him canned corn. The salesman had a convincing sales routine; he was especially proud of the fancy label on the can. Customers won't be able to resist it, he told Barney. "Might as well give the salesman's product a chance," he thought. "Let's see how it tastes." Young Barney had a small stove at the rear of his store where he brewed tea and tested products. As he walked to the back of his store, Barney tore off the colorful label and deliberately threw it on the floor. "My customers don't eat labels," he told the salesman, just to make a point. "They eat what's inside." Barney opened the can—it was full of hulls! He sent the salesman on his way without an order. Word spread and Barney's business grew.

After another year Barney bought out his partner, Branagan. A year later he opened three more stores. By 1893, there were 17 stores. Growth continued. Today, Barney Kroger's business is one of the largest retail grocery chains in the United States (Laycock, 1983).

Honesty Pays

My second story shows how policies of simple honesty and fairness can draw customers, lots of customers. At a time when fake medical cures, bordering on outright dishonesty, were prevalent, there was one magazine publisher who lived by the creed of only printing what he believed was true.

Cyrus Curtis was known as "the reformer in the marketplace." He was ahead of his time in that he refused to print misleading ads or advertise fraudulent medical cures. This he did even though he could have taken in hundreds of thousands of additional dollars in revenues had he chosen otherwise. Curtis wouldn't have anything to do with any product or any ad copy in which fraud or dangers to the product's user were present. This was partly a business decision but mostly it was based on his solid convictions about simple honesty.

Curtis believed that anything printed in his magazines reflected his character. And he felt that advertisements represented endorsements. If a product was advertised in the pages of his magazines, then it meant that he endorsed the product. To Cyrus Curtis, fraud was not just dishonest, it was also bad business. By refusing to accept questionable advertising, his readers came to trust what they read. As a consequence, those products that were trusted and did make their way into his publications, like *The Ladies Home Journal*, sold even better.

Business Knows the Importance of Integrity

Several years ago I received a letter from Carl Menk. At the time, Carl was chairman of Canny, Bowes, Inc., a prestigious executive search firm in New York City. He wrote to tell me about a survey his organization had recently conducted among senior executives to determine what attributes they considered important for executive leadership. They did not survey any executive whose name came out of a directory. Indeed not. This was a carefully planned piece of research. Carl's firm had tracked the career progress of over 1,000 senior level executives for many years. Only those who had demonstrated the greatest success were invited to participate. In a survey he asked these individuals to identify which characteristics were "very important," "important," or "less important" to success. After tabulating all the surveys, this is what they found: Integrity topped the list as the most important quality. It was followed by the ability to think conceptually and people skills. Decisiveness, intelligence, persuasiveness, and competitiveness were at or near the bottom of the list in terms of importance.

These findings were no fluke; others studying this question have arrived at exactly the same conclusion. A few years before Carl's study, Lester B. Korn of Korn Ferry, an internationally recognized executive search and consulting firm, undertook a similar study. In conjunction with UCLA's John E. Anderson Graduate School of Management, Korn surveyed a select group of senior executives. They were asked, "What quality do you think most necessary for business success?" Of 16 traits most responsible for enhancing an executive's chances for success, "integrity" topped the list. In fact, 71 percent of the senior executives surveyed said "integrity" was the most important quality.

How to Restore Integrity to the Workplace

Every time I am in San Francisco and drive across the Golden Gate Bridge, I see painters, busy at their trade. Their work never ends because just as soon as a fresh coat of paint is applied, the salt air persists with its relentless attack. Protecting the bridge from rust damage is an on-going battle. In a similar sense, all people and the organizations they work for need constant protection, too. Corrosive forces can attack and destroy the integrity of any workplace and render it ineffective and the people in it weak and unreliable. Restoring integrity to the workplace, like the continual upkeep of a bridge, involves constant attention.

Merely insisting that everyone tell the truth is not a bad idea, but it isn't a sufficient idea to achieve integrity in the workplace. Our life experiences tell us that a person's actions first run through his mind and before that they are played out in his heart, over and over. If the heart and mind are not right, one's actions will not be right either. This is a premise of this book and the reason why its chapters delve into matters of desire and beliefs and self-control. People everywhere have demonstrated the possibility that humans can become the kind of persons they choose to become. Those who succeed in crafting themselves into first-rate persons do so by both wanting and making right choices every day. They succeed at this because they examine their innermost desires with honesty and work to make their foremost wants admirable. This is a theme of the book: Integrity begins by thoughtful inspection of ourselves from within, from looking at what we honor and from looking at how we act.

Over the ages and in many places around the globe, thousands of people have distinguished themselves by the strength of their character. And you can, too. You can develop this remarkable inner quality that will bring about dramatic improvement—vital betterment in yourself, your work performance, your relations with others, and your business. This quality excites ordinary people to do great and worthwhile things and never complain about the hardships encountered along the way or expect praise for what they've done. It improves one's ability to decide wisely and interact with others effectively. And it saves people and organizations from lasting harm and shame. This quality always earns one the admiration of others. It is the common thread running through great lives, those we most admire. This remarkable quality is called integrity, and it's the steadfast practice of living up to high ideals. Many simply call it character.

CHAPTER 2

Develop Inner Strength

Cultivate the right dominating desires

You can always tell the caliber of a person by what ignites her interest. Once, while visiting one of our nation's finest art museums, I heard a woman remark to her companion, "I wonder how much all these paintings are worth?" After walking past and viewing these treasures by the masters, this appeared to be her foremost interest. One is left to wonder why she came to the art museum in the first place instead of walking along the docks of the local marina, where she could be impressed by the hefty price tags on the many fine, expensive yachts there. Her innermost concern, made evident by her question, was to fix a dollar value on treasures of vast intangible worth.

The inability to see and feel anything beyond the material and observable realm is widespread. If you doubt this, consider how frequently you hear someone say, as they see a craftsman's creation or an artist's work, or as they taste the culinary results of a skillful cook, "You should go into business. You could make a lot of money." Instead of delighting in the beauty of the artwork that they see or the tastes they enjoy, their thoughts center on only the tangible, the material, the market price. Their view of all that the world has to offer us is strikingly one-dimensional, extending no further than the monetary value needed to motivate exchange. Beyond that, their minds and hearts are unconcerned with anything else and incapable of understanding anything deeper.

Like a home, a human life has two aspects to it. It has an outside and an inside. From the street one can see a home's outside—its outer walls, its roof, its porch and chimney and windows. But enter inside and we find, dwelling there, much more than doors and cupboards and closets. We find deeper qualities running through the lives of those residing within. Most of what an alert and sensitive visitor would notice inside a house would center on the hospitality and the temperament and the range of concerns found in those who call this place home. In some homes the atmosphere is hostile, negative, bitter, and marked by sharp words, unkind thoughts, mean and hurtful acts. In other homes the atmosphere is strikingly different. It is peaceful, caring, loving. The difference all depends on what dominates the minds and hearts of those inside.

The outer life of a person consists of things we can see: body language, words, actions, creations, pleasures tasted, thoughts articulated, feelings expressed. A person's outer life involves connecting with the world and others in it. Some lives, on the outside, connect in many ways to many fine things, ideas, and persons. These lives we recognize as being alert, cultured, intelligent, clever, keen witted, knowledgeable of ideas and happenings, past and present. Other lives, on the outside, are rough and uncultured, slow to understand, unconcerned and disconnected from all except a few other people.

The inside of a life is difficult to probe. What goes on within the hidden interiors of a person—even ourselves—remains largely a mystery. Inner workings extend into realms beyond the powers of our perception, and there are qualities and dimensions beyond our worldly mind's ability to fully grasp. What we do know is that the inner life of a person is filled with dominating desires. These are the person's keenest concerns and burning drives, their loves and hates—all the forces that shape thought and animate action.

The secret to successful living is twofold. It involves having a well-developed outer life and a strong and vibrant inner life. We are two-dimensional creatures who are not happy, not secure, and not fully alive until our lives are awake to the seen and to the unseen. We need wide knowledge and varied experiences if we are ever to have a rich and fulfilling outer life. And, we need the depths of the world of enduring spiritual values to dominate our inner self to give us direction and stability as we adventure into the world and engage what we can see and touch in positive ways. No well-integrated life is possible without a fully developed outside, and inside, a realistic and sound connection to things visible and to things beyond vision and full human comprehension.

It is plainly evident from everyday experience that what happens on the inside of a person shapes what happens on the outside of that person. The direction and stability of a person's outer life are determined by what dominates the person's inner life. The greatest difficulties people face today do not arise from poorly developed outer lives but from impoverished inner lives. How else can we explain the meaninglessness that people experience and their inability to cope with life's greatest moments? The world we live in is filled with people who are keenly alert, worldly, mentally alive, and delightfully attuned to their surroundings. Yet many of these same people seem to fall to pieces when confronted with humanity's deepest moments and most crucial realities—birth, sin, triumph, suffering, failure, loneliness, joy, death. They haven't a clue as to how to meet them triumphantly. They are helpless. The reason is that their inner lives are vacuous, shallow, and adrift. They have no aim, no penetrating purpose beyond their own knowledge and status and possessions; they have little concern beyond self. There is no reverence, no root in anything that endures. What people need most is some invisible aim running through their inner lives, giving them a large and enduring purpose. They need something to grasp on to and be oriented by in the face of life's pains and pleasures. This is particularly important at a time when materialism is doing its best to convince them that the unseen is not real. Although difficult to achieve, it is within everyone's power to enrich their inner life, grounding it in eternal truths that do matter, that do endure, and that give humans the meaning and significance they so desperately crave but so often never fully find.

The world of work presents people with enormous challenges for strengthening their inner lives and great opportunities to make their outer lives full and rich. The workplace calls people to be more innovative, to create better methods and products, to be more service-oriented, to achieve better bottom-line results. These challenges require better knowledge than people have now, better working relationships than exist between themselves and others, and smarter strategies and plans than they have already devised. These are tall orders and people need all the strength and wisdom they can get to meet these demands. What people most need in their lives to do that is integrity—the essential element of a strong and well-developed inner life. The qualities of character that we see in those we regard most highly are the same qualities that enable people to perform effectively in the workplace. Conversely, the forces that diminish humans on the inside (greed, pride, hate, resentment, anger, jealousy) also make people less creative, less service-minded, and less reliable on the outside. The best way to strengthen peoples' ability to perform effectively, to achieve great things, is to strengthen inner-life qualities that make people good. The evidence for this claim lies in the biographies of those we most admire.

When we think of Mother Teresa, who followed her calling to minister to the lowest of the lowly in the worst slums of Calcutta, it is plainly evident that forces greater than self, namely serving a great calling, dominated her inner life. When we study the life of Jane Goodall, who became fascinated with chimpanzees and spent most of her life in remote sections of Africa studying these creatures in their natural habitat and thereby pioneered a new method of research, we see an inner life dominated by creative impulses and boldness and dedication to something far more enduring than earthly fame—she loved what she did and the primates she studied. When we think of Meriwether Lewis, who led one of the greatest expeditions our country has ever known, we see dominating in this man's inner life an intense desire to discover the wonders of the West and the integrity to follow scrupulously the scientific methods he learned from the best minds of his time.

Recognize a Dominant Desire

What can we say about two different CEOs of well-known, mega-size corporations, each on the brink of bankruptcy? One of these CEOs headed a discount retail chain. Outraged by what they saw going on, this company's employees wrote letters to the Securities and Exchange Commission reporting questionable accounting practices. Investigations followed. The whistle blowing forced the corporation to revise and reissue its income statement, reducing net reported earnings by over $100 million. But, following that, deeper problems surfaced. Investigators found that top management had secretly arranged for $28.9 million in retention loans for themselves. These loans, which did not require repayment, amounted to $5 million to the CEO and $3 million to his next-in-command. Vendors who had supplied goods already sold by the retail chain went unpaid, while the CEO received severance pay of $4 million (Thompson, Strickland, & Gamble, 2005).

The other CEO, the head of a major airline facing huge financial obligations, tried to keep his organization solvent just after the terrorist attacks of September 11, 2001. He realized that tens of millions of dollars were due within a week's time and he knew that his firm could not possibly cover these obligations immediately if something were not done. He went to his creditors and laid before them the facts as he knew them to be and asked for a few more days. He then rearranged his company's debt structure and, within a week, paid these obligations. But a deeper problem remained and he faced it head-on, too, with candor. The sad truth was that even if his firm could successfully reduce expenses by 20 percent, the airline would still incur losses of $200 million per month if passenger loads did not return to previous levels. Layoffs followed but this CEO and his next-in-command announced they would not accept their salary or bonuses for the remainder of the year. His employees supported him fully, and his airline continued flying passengers (Buthane, 1998). By establishing a climate of integrity himself, his employees, in turn, lived by higher motives and standards themselves.

The Tragedy of Having a Strong Outside and a Frail Inside

On a prominent corner in our town stands a giant oak tree. It has grown larger and more majestic over time. Experts tell us that it's well over one hundred and fifty years old but no one knows its exact age with certainty, because in our limited recall it has always been growing there. What we do know is that within recent memory it has withstood near hurricane-force winds, at least two lightning bolts, and numerous assaults from freezing rains whose ices of tremendous weight have snapped large limbs and felled less resolute growths. Yet, despite all of these assaults, the tree still stands. Sadly, this great specimen has become sickly looking and our local tree surgeon has rendered his diagnosis of the problem. Tiny insects have been eating away at this tree from the inside, weakening the integrity of its structure to the point that now it must be cut down before it topples and harms someone or causes damage. That is much the same way humans are toppled, not by assaults from without but by weakening attacks from within.

Several years ago *Business Week* reported a tragic situation. It involved a man named Don who got caught up in something that destroyed his career, himself, and, for a while, his company. In his early days it appeared that Don had everything it took to be successful in business. He had intelligence, imagination, and energy. Many people noticed in particular his drive to succeed. Don enjoyed a fortunate beginning in life, and he was an overachiever at an early age. He was born into a middle-class family in Middletown, New York. His father was a salesman for Gulf Oil. In high school Don played varsity football and basketball. He was known as a "big man on campus." At the University of Dayton, he was senior class president. Don graduated with a bachelor's degree in business in 1968, and then he went on to Syracuse University, where he earned an MBA. He had a strong outside and he knew it.

After that his career took off. His first job was with Bache & Company, as a stockbroker. While there he showed promise. Three years later he landed a job with a small Johnson & Johnson subsidiary called Jelco, which made catheters and syringes. Then in 1980, he joined a vacuum cleaner company, where he was made head of marketing. This company virtually owned the market for electric brooms but growth was slowing.

Don was known for his ambition. He put in long hours. Success was an ever-present concern—a subject he talked about continually. Some thought that Don was driven by a need to compete with his sister who was experiencing great financial success as a real estate broker, something he deeply envied. Regardless, Don's wife, Louise, described him as a "good, honest, sincere and loving man."

His success continued. Don brought good ideas to the firm, moving the vacuum cleaner company into higher-margin items. He promoted a new product, too: a carpet shampooer.

Don's ascent up the corporate ladder continued. It culminated in 1984 when he was named CEO. Dan was just 38 years old. Later that year, through a leveraged buyout from the parent firm, Dan took over his company. He held a 54 percent stake. Two years later his company went public.

Success continued. Don was a bit of a showman. At the first annual meeting, shareholders in attendance were treated to a model, clad in a bathing suit, sitting in a see-through bathtub, demonstrating his newest product: the home spa. It used the exhaust side of the vacuum motor to blow bubbles in water and create, for less than $100, the effect of a whirlpool. He also launched the "House-keeper," a competitor to the upright vacuum models of rival firms. Huge advertising expenditures pushed 1987 sales to $128 million, 68 percent over the previous year. Earnings grew 71 percent to $7.1 million.

Wall Street wanted its share, too. Its aim: to feed on investors' frenzy for a hot, growth company. Shearson Lehman promoted the firm's stock, informing investors in June 1988 that Don's company could grow by 50 percent in the next year alone. Analysts liked Don's style. The tall, stocky man, with dark curly hair, showed up at analysts' meetings in rumpled suits, shirt tails untucked. His intention was to "bomb" the industry leader, Hoover, something he indicated in a not very subtle way by placing a Hoover door mat on the orange carpet at the entrance to his office.

But this idea—walking over others—may also have been an early indication of the other Don, the one his co-workers and his employees saw. They saw a tough, aggressive boss. Some associates found him so abrasive that even when he was marketing vice president they discouraged him from making calls for fear he would offend customers. In his drive to grasp power and success for himself, he intimidated underlings. Turnover grew.

What fired Don's emotion more than anything else, it seems, was the company's stock price. By July 1988, it registered at a peak of $27\frac{1}{2}$, up from the $5\frac{1}{4}$ he paid in 1985. His stake in the company by then was worth a handsome $99 million. Don's compensation that year ran well over a half-million dollars, and he enjoyed it, living in a 12-room house on a 1.8-acre plot in upstate New Jersey. But trouble brewed.

Don's secretary tried out one of the first Housekeeper vacuums, only to find that the handle fell off when she lifted it. Also, the motor belt kept slipping off. Don didn't want to hear about it! Product returns swamped the company. More than 40,000 Housekeeper vacuums were returned in the third quarter of 1987 alone, 16 percent of sales. A separate warehouse was rented just to store them.

Don became desperate. In December 1987, he ordered his chief financial officer not to record the company's returned products. Later the CFO would say that he obliged his boss to keep his job. Stockbrokers were not aware of these difficulties; they continued to advise their clients to "buy."

The pattern of deception continued. In 1988 Don ordered the firm's accountants to "cook the books." Specifically, they were to come up with sales of $180 million and per-share earnings of $1.20. Their solution was to book a sale when an order was received instead of when it was shipped. This put an additional $6 million into sales in the fourth quarter. Expenses were understated—to the tune of $3 million. Two hundred fake invoices were generated by the firm's computer, worth another $5.4 million. This, it was later revealed, came about during the last 3 days of 1987.

Wall Street, perhaps because of greed, remained fooled—not even suspicious! They continued advising their clients: "Buy." The board members were hood-winked, too. Some were concerned by the fact Don didn't produce numbers, but his smooth talking overcame their trepidations.

The bubble was about to burst. And, on Tuesday, September 20, 1988, it finally did. It was no use—the situation was so bad and out of control. At the board meeting that day, Don broke down and cried. He told directors the company would report substantially lower earnings. A day later stock prices went from 17 to $7\frac{1}{8}$. Shearson Lehman yanked the company's stock from its preferred list. Angry investors and analysts jammed the telephone lines to Don's office. He refused to take all but a few of the over 100 daily calls from irate investors.

Over the weekend Don confessed all to his wife and then to his priest. On Monday he resigned. A week later he made a full confession to the U.S. attorney in Newark. He was sent to prison for a year. As a result of the fraud, the company folded. The huge complex that once employed hundreds was bolted shut and employees found themselves without jobs.

The Practice of Cooking the Books

John E. Anderson, a prominent business and civic leader in Los Angeles, urged me recently to say something in this book about the problem of dishonest accounting. (In 1987, UCLA renamed its Graduate School of Management the John E. Anderson School of Management in honor of his accomplishments and contributions to the school.) Dishonest accounting isn't a new phenomenon, but the dollar amounts are ever so much greater today than they were in the past that the problem has grown much larger and severe. There can be little doubt that in many instances within corporate America, greedy instincts have won out over better judgment. This is especially noticeable when we examine how pressures for better bottom-line results have moved accountants to bend the rules and misrepresent their organization's financial health and past performance. To better understand the nature of this problem we need to go into the minds and hearts of those who are on the firing line day after day, responsible for meeting the expectations of higher-ups. Imagine the person charged with reaching clearly established performance targets. At the extreme, her job is on the line. But more often than not it is a year-end bonus that hangs in the balance, or a much-wanted raise or promotion. And there is always the ego and its wants. Pride causes people to do all kinds of things to look good and gain favor from others. So naturally people try to make it appear that they are meeting or exceeding expectations. Any organization can easily mislead individuals into doing things they should not do whenever it places too much pressure on employees to achieve results they are incapable of achieving.

The dangers at the individual level are even more pronounced at the corporate level. Investors expect earnings to be high and grow rapidly. They want to see strong sales increases and tight control on expenses. So, with their jobs and bonuses and stock options riding in the balance, corporate leaders are frequently tempted to pressure accountants to "cook the books," to "make the numbers" to get earnings to where Wall Street will be pleased, its analysts impressed. And it's here where accountants are tempted to overestimate the true value of assets, book sales that are dubious, and underestimate expected merchandise returns and warranty expenses. There are so many areas where judgment calls and estimates must be made. Despite the accounting profession's standards aimed at promoting honesty, the forces acting on corporate executives at the top of an organization have a way of pressuring them to not tell the true story, to falsify financial statements. The importance of transparency, of reporting how estimates and judgments were made, becomes apparent when we look for ways of preventing this kind of misrepresentation. But in the end, the surest antidote is the individual's commitment to telling the truth, placing it ahead of today's rewards.

The Destructiveness of Greed

Don had a comfortable income, no doubt. But that didn't satisfy him; it wasn't enough. He wanted still more. And the tragic thing about Don was that the more he got, the more he wanted. And his wants grew larger than his self-control and sense of proportion: whatever he had was never sufficient. He always wanted more. The temptations from his outer life were stronger that the strengths of his inner life.

Greed begins its trickery, first by getting us to think we can't get along without what we want. And once we achieve that, it continues to whisper in our hearts, clamoring for more, demanding not to be disappointed. And, finally, it twists our judgment, convincing us that it's okay to use whatever means it takes to reach our desires—because, after all, we deserve it. The ancient Romans expressed it this way: Greed is like sea water. The more you drink, the thirstier you become.

No life is whole until a person develops the capacity to see beyond the material realm and his or her own well-being. The secret of the selfish person is that all masterful and controlling wants extend no farther than their pocketbook or stomach. Nothing is so desirable to this sort of person than to be safe and fortunate themselves.

It's the Doing that Matters

The surest defense against greed's devastating treachery can be found in the lives of men and women whom we most admire for their qualities of character. Suppose a famous personality came into a restaurant and put up a tremendous fuss, making a scene and being a nuisance. Imagine the celebrity demanding special treatment, complaining about the food and service, and acting rudely to the help. What are we to conclude? Yes, the entertainer is talented and widely known, and probably very rich. The point is that what a person has—talents, fame, wealth—is not the same as who that person is. While it's well understood that every normal person wants to feel important, to be someone deserving of admiration and respect, it's also true that people can try to reach these aims by different routes. The chief difference between those we admire and those we cannot admire generally lies in the fact that the former gauge their self-worth in terms of what they do and the latter in terms of what they have.

Several years ago I traveled across the United States, interviewing successful business leaders, CEOs of our country's largest and most profitable companies. It is no secret that these leaders earn handsome incomes. Out of curiosity I asked each of them the same question: "What has given you the greatest satisfaction in your life?" Many of them talked about their families. Many spoke of how they helped their companies grow and prosper. Many told of being in the right place at the right time to make a positive difference in the lives of others. And a few talked with pride about how they rescued their organizations from financial ruin and made it possible for thousands of employees to retain their jobs. But not one of them said, "I got rich and could afford this or that expensive luxury." The point is that these achievers were successful because they chose to give their finest efforts to building something worthwhile. They are far more interested in doing things than they are in having things. The inner strength they seem to have is the ability to focus their thoughts and energies on doing, not having.

Learn to Master Your Belongings

It takes a strong inner life to conquer greed and master one's belongings, and not be mastered by them. If you think about it, all our lives we seem to be learning how to grow smarter and more skillful at getting things. Yet once we achieve these aims, we find ourselves helpless, like small children lost in a strange city. We are unable to master what we own, and we are without the strength to not be mastered by it. I was a guest once at a dinner party given by one of the leading industrialists in Cincinnati and his wife. Their modest home, perched on a hillside, offered a splendid view of the Ohio River. But other than that, it was what most people would consider to be an ordinary, older home. It was stately, but it wasn't lavish. Make no mistake about it; these people could easily afford a much bigger, a much more spectacular home. Yet they choose to live inconspicuously, far more modestly than do most others at their level of wealth.

I think they chose to live this way because they wanted to use their personal wealth for things they considered to be more important than extravagancies. They wanted to use what they had—and it was substantial—to build something worthwhile and lasting, something they thought was far more important than enjoying luxuries that they knew they could do without.

Over the years this man and his wife have made major contributions to the arts and to educational institutions. They are far more interested in building for the future than they are with consuming in the present. Simply put, they know how to master their money, using it for causes they want to see succeed, causes that will continue on for many years, and after they are gone. Their money is not mastering them, turning them into people they would not choose to be. They appear to have have an unbelievable kind of enthusiasm for what they do, a steadiness with a sense of conviction behind it. I believe they have this marvelous inner quality because they are engrossed in building up their community, using what they have in terms of money and talent to do it.

Conrad Hilton (Hilton, 1957), of Hilton Hotel fame, spoke of the dangers of getting too tied to one's belongings. He advised, "Don't let your belongings possess you. They are very nice to have, to enjoy, to share. But if you find one you can't live without, hasten to give it away. Your freedom depends on it." Hilton illustrated this idea in his book *Be My Guest* with a story about a monkey. A monkey puts his hand through a narrow mouth jar to grasp a desired object. Then he tries to pull it out, but he can't. The fist he has made grasping what he wants makes the monkey's hand too large to be withdrawn. So, the monkey is stuck and the poor thing is too stupid to let go of what he holds and be free. So, too, it is with humans. We, likewise, trap ourselves whenever we grasp for much larger prizes, things that are too big to fit into a small jar, and are too foolish to let go.

A very useful power, this is—mastering what one owns. I once heard about a man who purchased a rare and expensive violin. It cost him hundreds of thousands of dollars, but the expense was of little concern to him because he was fabulously wealthy. In fact, he had far more wealth than he knew how to spend wisely. Now the sad part of this story is that he didn't know how to play the violin, nor did he know anyone with sufficient talent who could unleash the remarkable sounds that this wonderful instrument was capable of producing. This man bought the violin just so he could boast of owning it. And because of that, the remarkable instrument went unused; it was never played. What could have been used to produce incredibly beautiful music, if placed in the right hands, became a showpiece, something to gratify this man's ego.

There seems to be a law of life that says the more wealth one has, the wiser and more disciplined one must be in order to use that wealth effectively. Owning something and using something are vastly different things. It takes someone of enormous imagination and good sense and character to be able to use great wealth in great ways. Having vast material wealth is neither good nor bad in itself. It all comes down to how one uses what one has. That's the key. Are possessions put to useful ends—to build, to uplift, to add beauty and abundance? Are they really being enjoyed as they function in their intended purposes? Or are they merely held to flatter one's ego or used to prevent boredom for the lack of having anything else to do?

I once had a very enlightening conversation with a remarkable man named Douglas Danforth. It took place the morning of his last day of work, before he retired as chairman and CEO of Westinghouse in Pittsburgh. On that day he could look back on his long and distinguished business career with a good bit of wisdom gained from his many years of experience. Naturally, I was keenly interested in learning what he had to say. One of the things we discussed was how he viewed wealth and the challenges it presents to those who have it.

The first thing he told me was that most of the senior executives at Westinghouse—and I'm sure it's true at other companies, too—came from modest beginnings. Most senior executives of his generation had to work their way through college. He said that those who struggled in their early years to succeed tended not to lose track of that part of their lives. The experience taught them that the greatest satisfaction is derived through working hard to achieve something worthwhile. And it is the experience itself—the struggle, not the tangible outcomes that come from it—that is the real reward, a reward that is most satisfying.

Then he told me something that I found fascinating. He said that, of course, top executives of publicly held companies are paid very well. Yet, he said, most choose not to live at a standard their income could support. That may sound surprising, but they do that for a couple of reasons. For one, material things become superfluous after a while. You have a new car and a nice home and fine clothes and you take nice vacations. But beyond that, overspending can bring troubles. Few people need a yacht or an airplane, which can be very expensive. High living can be troublesome. It just isn't good for people.

The other reason is that, as thoughtful parents, they don't want their children to grow up in an artificial cocoon. One can grow up with the country club set, living in the lap of luxury, and become useless because of it. Parents who give their children too much can deprive them of something that's vitally important to building strong inner lives. And that is the chance to learn how to dig success out for one's self.

Red Adair, the man who made a name for himself by putting out oil field blazes—his firm was called on to extinguish the fires in Kuwait after the Iraqi army was beaten back—was no stranger to this important truth. He put it this way: "Life isn't having it made; it's getting it made. Each necessary task requires an effort of will, and with each act something in you grows and is strengthened."

Focus on Building

There's another weapon available to us in the battle against the forces of greed that can impoverish one's inner life. It is the ability to focus attention on building—developing a new technology, increasing customer loyalty, improving product quality, making an organization better able to perform its work. I am speaking of building, here, in the broadest sense. It includes creating ideas and objects of worth, functional and aesthetic—whatever adds abundance and improves conditions. These can be big or small—it makes little difference qualitatively. The idea is to add something positive to the world.

People are made better when they realize that building does not alone result in the creation of objects and structures and improvements. It also makes them into the persons they are. In truth, we are what we do, not what we have. And through each of our accomplishments, our inner lives tend to grow stronger, our ability to experience the spiritual dimensions becomes keener. It's the doing, not the having, that makes life large and brings satisfaction and a sense of significance. Thomas Monaghan became a multimillionaire through building the Domino's Pizza chain. One day in 1980, he went to see Ray Kroc, the man who made McDonald's into the world's largest chain of restaurants. Monaghan saw Kroc as an entrepreneurial genius, and he tried to emulate him. While sitting in Mr. Kroc's office chatting, Kroc said to Monaghan, "Tom, you've got it made now. So play it safe. Open a few stores every year, but don't make any deals that could get you into trouble."

Monaghan was shocked. He couldn't believe that the entrepreneur he so admired would say such a thing—it defied what he thought Kroc believed in. Unable to restrain himself, Monaghan blurted out, "But that wouldn't be any fun!"

A long, silent pause gripped the room. Then, a big grin appeared on Kroc's face as he jumped to his feet and walked around his desk to shake Monaghan's hand. "That's just what I hoped you'd say!" (Anderson, 1990).

CHAPTER 3

Respect Deep-Seated Feelings

Listen to your inner voice

No explanation of how people develop consistent patterns of integrity in their outer lives can be anywhere near complete without an understanding of how they can connect with their inner lives. It has long been recognized that humans live in two worlds: the seen and the unseen. Their lives have an outside and an inside. The outer life of a person is observable, and it includes the material realm. The inner life involves spiritual forces that shape thoughts, feelings, and actions. To be sure, humans dignify their existence by exercising their thinking capabilities and by developing their minds. Likewise, they ennoble their lives when they regard seriously their feelings and those forces within their personality that influence their actions. There can be little doubt that humans are capable of living in realms beyond the physical, the observable. And when they do, they can grow richer in spirit. This involves understanding what's taking place within the hidden depths of their inner lives and nurturing their spiritual centers therein. An outstanding ability humans have is their capacity to connect with their inner lives—they can hear the urgings coming from their spiritual centers. This amazing quality gives them a certain level of mastery over themselves.

The Inner Voice

Individuals from every age and every land have reported experiencing the presence of something that speaks to them from somewhere within the hidden depths and mysteries of their "self." This experience is something like hearing a small voice that calls to them from their inner being. It speaks not so much in words but in the universal language of emotions and in more subtle ways yet— guiding, inspiring, energizing, prodding, consoling, directing, and warning them.

The conscience, something everyone reports feeling, is part of this inner voice, but there is more to it than that alone. The inner voice also connects us to our powers of emotion, creativity, reason, and judgment. Functioning as it ought, this remarkable inner voice sometimes works much like a homing signal that guides airplanes safely through storms and thick fogs. This inner voice connects our outer life with our inner self, our inner spirit—our whole invisible personality that thinks, loves, and animates actions. It allows us the possibility to increase our awareness of our spiritual center, in all its heights and depths.

Our inner voice "speaks" to us in mysterious ways. Yet, what it tells us can be unmistakably clear if we but develop the capacity to listen. It can tell us many important things about ourselves and what we might choose to do with our lives. For example, we might find that we are best suited to certain pursuits. This is our inner voice at work. We might become inspired by another person's actions, like their compassion or bravery or love. This, too, is our inner voice, speaking to us. Perhaps it might tell us that we ought to act like a person we admire. These are logical dimensions of our inner voice. It has emotional dimensions, too. We might, if only momentarily, become overwhelmed with feelings of deep joy or intense delight when we accomplish something or when we see a beautiful sunset or powerful waterfall. We might become choked up with emotion and find ourselves unable to speak. These also are the workings of our inner voice, speaking to us. But why should we listen to it? Why should we try to understand what it says and respond to its call?

Many think the inner voice experience should be taken seriously because they believe it, like every other human function, serves some useful purpose. When they consider what exists in the world, they observe that everything exists for a reason. This appears to be the case with humans; each part of the body plays a role. Each part performs some vital function: eyes to see and guide, hands to touch and grasp, legs to carry us about, lungs to breathe, brain to think. It is also obvious that humans have emotions, too. Our fear, our pride, our joy, our lust, our hatred, our love—all these emotions—serve useful purposes. Surely, the inner voice experience that humans have serves a useful purpose, too. Many wise people who have considered this matter carefully believe that the inner voice arises out of our inner spirit. And they believe each person's inner spirit exists to make that person more fully alive, more fully human.

Calls from Within

One way to obtain deeper insights into the nature of our inner voice is to consider how it affects ordinary people doing everyday things. For example, an experience commonly reported by men and women of science runs something like this. The scientist patiently proceeds through one experiment after another, looking for a breakthrough. All possible avenues for a solution have been tried—at least that's what his intellect tells him. Yet, his inner voice, calling from within, urges him onward: "Keep trying; there is still another avenue of investigation that will lead you to a solution that you believe will come. Don't stop now."

The scientist knows that it would be easy to call a halt to his research. Countless others have already tried unsuccessfully to unlock the mystery he seeks to unlock. No one would think ill of him if he did stop now. But he cannot bring himself to do that. Not just yet. The scientist's boss is beginning to grow impatient with him and urges him to move on to something else. But the scientist's inner voice urges him to stick with his investigation, for just a little bit longer. For some reason each avenue that leads to a dead end also presents the scientist with another idea, another possible route to the answer he seeks. It is this continuation of on-going possibilities born out of failures that seeds his inner voice with an insistent urging for him to continue on, to not quit now.

One of the most important questions people frequently ask themselves is, "Am I doing what I ought to be doing?" What they want to know is whether they are pursuing something that they ought to be pursuing, something that's right for them. The conscience, which the inner voice experience includes, is generally reliable in warning us when we are doing things we should not to be doing. But a larger concern is whether we are doing what we should be doing. Many people are sincerely concerned with whether they are fulfilling those purposes that they were meant to fulfill, using their unique qualities and talents. Too many people today are doing things they think they should be doing out of misplaced guilt or the lust of material possessions and they are miserable because of it. Yet, their inner voice persists in trying to tell them as much. The problem these people have is that they don't know how to interpret or trust what their inner voice says. The best way to know whether one is "on track," doing what he or she is well-suited to do, is the presence of an unmistakably strong feeling of intense joy and a lasting sense of satisfaction. We may come to a point in life where we are afraid to move in a new direction and fear giving up what's known and comfortable. But until a decision is made and actual steps are taken, no one can tell whether the new direction is right. If it is right for a person, then, like a gyroscope, that person will feel in balance when continuing in that pursuit and will feel out of sorts when straying from it.

Unseen Realities

We might just as well face squarely here, at the outset, the possibility that there is no such thing as an inner voice phenomenon at all. Certainly we cannot photograph it, or measure its length, or calculate its mass. It won't register on a decibel meter. It is entirely conceivable that the cynics of the world are correct: this thing we call our inner voice might merely be a product of our imaginations and our hopes that there is more to us as humans than our physical bodies. Maybe this voice can be explained away as nothing more than our stomach's reaction to an extra helping of last night's pizza. Perhaps, what we believe our own thoughts to be are nothing more than random movements of brain cells in a sea of chemicals producing electric impulses.

The deficiency of this explanation is that it is inconsistent with our experience. Consider the kinds of actions we know to exist: A person feels remorse for making a mistake and says, "I'm sorry. I won't let it happen again." Another person is unwilling to quit in the middle of what appears to be an impossible task and keeps going in the face of difficulties because of a gnawing drive to keep going. Another person creates a work of art that is aesthetically pleasing to millions. This work of art did not arise immediately and after just a few minutes of work. Rather it evolved slowly and demanded considerable work and re-work until something spoke from within the creator of it saying, "This feels right; it is aesthetically pleasing now." Another person forms new ideas and writes them down because there is a sense that the ideas are valuable. Another person examines evidences and changes a long-held view because the facts logically lead to an opposite conclusion; something inside this person says that the truth matters more than one's pride. How impossible is it for us to believe that such actions are without an explainable source, that they are mere chance events. Surely something is going on in the inside of these people that explains their actions.

It is entirely within the realm of possibilities that our universe includes dimensions that humans are incapable of perceiving with their senses. Were we not equipped with eyes, how else would we know that sight is possible? If we did not have ears, how would we know that sound exists? It is a distinct possibility that there may be another dimension that we do not know of, because we do not have a sense mechanism to perceive it. Curiously, our minds are capable of conceiving the possibility of such a dimension. Humans have always been intrigued with the possibility that something else is going on within and around them that they cannot see, taste, smell, hear, or feel by touch. Some thinkers hypothesize that humans may evolve, some day, to the point where they acquire another sense, allowing them access to a next dimension. But for now, our limited abilities can only suspect something is happening within humans. Exactly what that is—some call it the inner spirit—we can only guess.

We do know that something deep within humans is alive and at work. If one were to sprinkle iron filings over a sheet of paper and slide a magnet around underneath it, the tiny bits of metal would move about. An observer seeing only what's visible on the surface would discern the movements of the filings but would not see the cause. If we were to leave the magnet in place and gingerly vibrate the paper, the iron filings would jiggle about in no discernible pattern at first. But after a short while a pattern would emerge out of the randomness. The tiny filings would align themselves in the direction of the magnet's field. They would become magnetized themselves and point toward the magnet's poles.

Like the force of magnetism acting on the tiny filings, there is a great, unseen power alive in humans. It may not move their physical bodies as directly as a truck pulls a trailer, but it does influence their wills to choose. Breaking through the material realm, there is a force within us that reveals itself through our thoughts, our emotions, and our actions. It is our inner spirit. Our inner spirit speaks its desires through our inner voice, an impulse that cautions us, awakens us, drives us onward, and won't let us rest easy until we yield to its call. And that call beckons us to be more fully alive, more fully human, more creative, more loving.

Calls that Create Progress

Like the magnet that mysteriously moves tiny iron filings, our inner voices call us to move our lives in directions that improve the human condition. That this is happening is made abundantly clear by the fact of human progress: progress in terms of material abundance, in terms of intelligent thought, in terms of social order and harmony among peoples of the world, in terms of advancements in knowledge and technology, in terms of aesthetic expression. Despite backward strides that shock and sadden us, the human condition is improving because men and women have listened to their inner voices. It is true that we once lived in caves, practiced cannibalization, offered human sacrifices. It is true that we once tolerated slavery, exploited children, tarnished our environment. It is true that we've exterminated fellow human beings and that we continue to do so. But it is also true that those who inhabit our world are causing the human condition to progress in ways thoughtful minds see as better: greater material abundance, more freedoms, advances in science and technology, more creative expression in literature and the arts, safer environments, improved health, greater respect for human rights and the sanctity of life. The list is long.

The important point to bear in mind is that this thing called human progress arises out of a force far deeper than just rational thought and purposeful action. That force is allowed to work on us through our inner voice impulses. That force is the human inner spirit. It is the source of all our desires, of our will to act, our humanity. The workings of inner spirit forces have a God-like quality to them. They appear to be oriented toward some great purpose. At its basic level this force is best recognized as a person's resolute will to take charge of self and make something of it. It is the act of grappling with one's life, something that you have observed in others and struggle with every day yourself.

That we can think and know that we do think is evidence itself that our thoughts are the product of something more than random chemical reactions. That we respond to our finer impulses is evidence that our inner spirits exist to make us more useful, more creative, more likeable—if we but allow them to work their magic on our lives. That we find ourselves experiencing uplifting emotions like joy, trust, and love whenever we act in ways that make us more human is evidence that our inner voice speaks to us through our emotions. And that we find ourselves experiencing uncomfortable and unbearable emotions like shame, regret, and sorrow when we act in ways that make us less human and when we degrade the human condition is evidence that our inner voices also exist to call us to goodness.

To better explain this idea, consider the following situation. A man travels along a country road and spots an accident. Another driver has crashed. It appears to be serious. The man pulls over and calls the local police. He looks inside the victim's car and sees someone slumped over the steering wheel. He opens the door and checks the victim's breathing and pulse. He applies a compress to stop the bleeding. Our "Good Samaritan" comforts the victim and waits until help arrives.

If we were to look at this event through the eyes of a scientist, we would see a large, moving object made of metal, rubber, and glass come to rest near another metal, rubber, and glass object. Then a mass of flesh with hair and nearly completely covered with different pieces of cloth would emerge from one of the metal, rubber, and glass objects and move toward the other one. We would then hear sounds coming from the flesh-like mass. We would see the obvious. But this is not all that is taking place.

Behind the material realm, with its architecture of physical forces and rational thought, there is another realm, with its own architecture of purposes and forces. These forces lie deeper than knowledge of what to do. These are the forces of the inner spirit; and they include things like a sense of duty, a feeling of responsibility, the respect for reason, the desire to create, and human compassion. These forces animate one's desire to create and to use knowledge, to care for others, to allow one's will to dictate behaviors.

Forces of the Inner Life

One important aspect of the inner life of humans involves the fact that their spiritual centers can host a wide range of spiritual forces, both good and evil, all at the same time. Our race regards as good those eternal values that make us more decent, more honest, more loving, more sincere and hard-working. These spiritual forces fully awaken our capacities as persons and elevate the quality of our existence. Evil spiritual forces include things like slothfulness, anger, pride, envy, lust, which make us small, mean, unable to contribute productively, or live in harmony with others. No one knows better than our selves the difficulties that can erupt within whenever some of the forces in our inner lives battle other ones, as each tries to dominate our outer life.

It is worth mentioning that whenever a spiritual force, good or ill, dominates an aspect of our outer life long enough, it will develop a strong hold on that aspect of us. To get a crude idea of what this involves, imagine a small iron rod placed across the ends of a powerful, horseshoe-shaped magnet. If left there for awhile, something noticeable begins to happen within it. The powerful force field of the magnet aligns the electrons in the atoms that make up the small iron rod. After a time, the rod itself becomes magnetized, with a positive charge on one end and a negative charge on the other. In a similar fashion, the outer lives of humans can become oriented by the powerful forces of their spiritual centers. And the nature of our outer actions depends on which forces dominate us within.

Stability

It would be far from true to say that the inner spirit found in humans is fluid, that it is easily changed by whatever forces blow. It would be closer to the truth to say that our spiritual centers have a kind of built-in resistance to unwholesome values. Our spiritual centers tend to call us to be dominated by what we consider to be good forces, and they want to keep it that way. It is as if our spiritual centers try to maintain themselves in good operating order by signaling to us through feelings of unease when we behave badly, when evil forces dominate our desires. These experiences suggest that a person's inner spirit is not without powers and resilience of its own. And many people believe that even greater powers still are alive and at work trying to influence each person's inner spirit. As a crude way to illustrate the idea that the human spirit tends to want to find a state of stability, that it seeks to have itself dominated with good forces that keep the outer life in balance, imagine a gyroscope in operation. You probably played with a toy one as a child and can recall how the large, heavy wheel, spinning about on an axis, held the gyroscope in a balanced position. You could place it on a string or wire stretched tight, or on the point of a pencil, and it would not topple over. If the mass of the rotating wheel were greater, according to the laws of physics, or if its velocity were increased, its stability would, correspondingly, become greater, too.

This simple device depicts, in principle, the basic idea of what happens when the human spirit—like the operating gyroscope—is functioning under the influences of good forces. Now, let bad forces act on the inner spirit, trying to seize control of the forces that keep our outer life in balance. If they come upon our inner spirit with sufficient force, as one might give the spinning instrument a heavy-handed spank, they will throw our outer lives off balance. But push on the gyroscope slightly or blow at it with heavy breath, and it resists. There is something like this going on within each human's inner life, in the inner spirit. Like a gyroscope, we run well on the outside—in our outer life—as we are meant to run, when we are balanced. And, like the gyroscope, the inner spirit of a human life has inner powers of resistance to unwholesome spiritual forces that upset lives. The more good forces we allow to dominate our inner lives, the better balanced we become.

I want to continue with the gyroscope example to make one more point. Imagine yourself holding the spinning instrument in your hand. Now, imagine what happens when you twist your hand, tipping the gyroscope from side to side. You feel resistance. The spinning wheel wants to continue moving in its original plane and it "tells you so." You feel the resistance. This is something like what happens to us as our inner spirit speaks though our inner voice. We have a sensation. It isn't a verbal message, yet it is unmistakably a message—one that we feel.

The Divine Within

There is yet another quality about our inner voice, perhaps the most wonderful quality of all. It is true: we all have flaws and weaknesses. We act on desires that shame us. We can be rude to others to get our point across. We can be less than honest in trying to get someone else do what we want them to do. We can skip out on our commitments. We can shirk our responsibilities. We can think of ourselves and only ourselves when the pressure to perform is intense or the competition is fierce. Yet, however despicable and unlovely we may be, our inner voice never abandons us. It never writes us off, never gives up hoping for our betterment, never stops trying to call us to be better persons than we are. Our inner voice is exceedingly patient with us. It takes no offense at our determined indifference to it. Like a loving parent will do when a child strays onto wayward paths, our inner voice urges us to "come home," to reunite with the family, to be lovable once again. Indeed, there is a godly nature to our inner spirit. St. Augustine best captured the idea when he stated, "Thou, O God, hast made us for thyself and we are restless until we find ourselves in thee" (St. Augustine, 354–430 A.D.).

The divine takes up residence in our inner spirit, and we realize from our experience that one cannot find rest until our inner spirit has integrity. Taken together, our thoughts, feelings, and actions are the working of the inner spirit. When our thoughts, feelings, and actions are unified by the wonderful strengths of the inner spirit, the voice within us speaks in ways we find satisfying, fulfilling, exhilarating. But when we are not unified, our inner voice speaks in ways that we find painful. More wondrously, it is a voice of unmistakable strength and wisdom.

The inner voice within us is not of our own making. We did not create it to please ourselves. We did not, as a playwright does, create the script it speaks. And so, unexpectedly, ideas come to us that we cannot explain. We are uneasy about the quality of what we are making until we feel we have made it right, our standards have been met. We find intense joy in expressing our creativity, in doing things we intuitively understand as being "us." We hear a call for our time and service, a call to which we cannot say, "No." These are inner voice experiences. Our inner voice is a gift, a gift worth using.

Hearing the Voice and Responding to Its Call

This creative and caring force, our inner voice, calls out to us in ways that defy description and rational understanding. Only when our minds and hearts are still are we capable of faintly perceiving this power. It influences us in subtle ways, not by words but through impulses of deeper realizations of things lasting and true. The inner voice exists in a realm beyond what our five senses can ordinarily perceive. As if coming from the innermost chambers of the heart, this inner voice phenomenon whispers to us faintly, continually. But our hearing it is not as faithful as are its outreaching calls to us. Preoccupation with problems and the pressures of daily living grab for our attention, disconnecting our conscious mind from its inner presence. One of the most striking features of the inner voice is that it never demands. It does not shout. It does not intrude on our thoughts with the same force of insistency that the daily concerns of our busy lives have a way of doing. Instead, the inner voice quietly but persistently invites one's attention, one's respect.

Difficult to decipher, the inner voice tries to guide our choices, direct our lives, order our actions, and cause us to take responsibility for who we are and what we could become. The inner voice, when operating effectively, does not cower in the face of unwholesome wants and deeds. It can be the source of troublesome feelings of shame, causing something deep within us to ache. At other times it fills us with something that could b st be described as overwhelming joy and exhilaration. Regardless of the feelings that the voice evokes, experience suggests that our limited minds and powers of perception will forever be inadequate to comprehend the fullness of meaning of what it says.

Practically all accomplished persons are known to take seriously calls from their inner voice. Everyone would do well to learn better how to understand it and become more patient in trying to listen to it carefully and follow its urgings. Through listening to our inner voice we can find our unique passions, the purposes we were created to pursue. When we hear our inner voice and heed its urgings, we thereby live more purposeful lives. And so, a young boy who likes reading books grows up. He reads and he delights in thinking about what he reads. He talks to others about the things he reads and finds satisfaction in that, too. He wonders if it might be possible to make reading and discussing ideas his life's work. His love of reading and thinking lead him to take his schooling seriously. He performs well. His parents want him to take over the family business but his heart isn't in that. Despite their urgings to pursue their desires for him, he chooses to follow his own dreams. He goes to college and on to further study after that. He becomes a teacher.

Another person is employed by a large organization that goes through difficult times. The company's top management faces wrenching decisions that affect hundreds of good employees. They must be terminated if the company is to survive. This person is deeply affected by these painful events and sees a need for employee training and the application of better management methods to prevent future occurrences of this kind of tragedy. Her inner voice says, "You should use your knowledge and experience to prevent such things from happening to others." She becomes a consultant to other companies, providing them with creative approaches to employee development processes and improved management practices.

A man finds he has a problem with another man in his organization. The two become rivals and cannot get along. The first man's inner voice tells him, "This is not good. It isn't good for your company. It isn't good for the other person. It isn't good for you." He regrets his unkind words and nasty deeds. They sicken him. So, the man vows that he will rise above his pettiness and small-minded squabbling. He turns to his pastor for counseling. He reads books. He prays. He talks to friends. He changes himself, becoming more tolerant, less judgmental, less hostile, less aggressive. By responding to his inner voice and by changing what's inside of himself, he becomes a changed man on the outside. His relationship with his rival improves. He works more effectively with others. Even his home life gets better.

These are the kinds of changes that are possible when one lives in two worlds. By listening to their inner voices, these three people changed. They became richer in spirit because they heard their inner voice and acted on what they heard. But hearing one's inner voice is no simple matter. Listening to the longings coming from the inner spirit takes skill, a skill that requires disciplined practice to develop fully. Sadly, that practice is rarely undertaken. It's not because we are incapable of practice; it's because we allow ourselves to be diverted from our inner voices by everyday distractions and pressures. We tune out our inner voices. These many distractions become our convenient excuses.

The Language of the Inner Voice

How does one know the language of his or her inner voice? While we cannot be entirely sure, we can be reasonably confident that it is a voice that causes our innermost emotions to reverberate with joy, interest, and confidence, giving us a level of vigor unlike anything else we have ever experienced. It can also be a voice that speaks to us in terms of success and failures and how we choose to define success and failure—whether one defines it to be getting what he or she sets out to obtain, or whether one sees it as personal growth and improvement gained by the lessons learned from succeeding or failing.

One useful guide to hearing our own inner voice is to pay attention to ourselves and accept our uniqueness. We hear our unique voices in very different ways because we are unique individuals. Some of us are inclined musically. At church services, for instance, some people will be moved by the music, others by the recitation of prayer, others by the thoughts contained in the sermon. Some people connect with their inner voice through visual experiences, others through their intellect. A view of the Pacific Ocean can be a moving experience to one man, while the intricacies of a scientific principle will be a deeply emotional experience for another.

Because we are not alike, we hear differently; we thereby hear different things and are uplifted, tormented, challenged, and changed by different events. This is part of a larger plan whereby each human has a role to play, a role that each person is uniquely equipped to perform. And, the human condition will be shaped for better or worse by how each individual responds to his or her inner voice.

Forces that Deafen Us to Our Inner Voice

The world is filled with many forces, some inside us and others outside that work to disconnect us from our inner lives. We do well to know what these enemies are and how they operate, and to not underestimate their destructive capabilities.

- Self-avoidance: This enemy tries to convince us that we are too busy right now to stop and listen to our inner voice. It tells us, "Maybe later, when there's more time; but not just now."

- Forced goals: This enemy makes us so concerned with reaching our career targets that we are unwilling to consider unfolding opportunities for our lives and calls from our inner voice urging us to move in new directions.

- Faulty self-perception: This enemy keeps us from knowing our real abilities and interests by having us do other things, using other talents, so as to please others and to win their flattery.

- Gossipy delights: This enemy wants us to focus our minds on little things having little significance instead of big things that matter more to our lives.

- Guaranteed rewards: This enemy deafens us to our inner voice when it calls us to do things that require slightly more talent than we may have when starting out on an enterprise. This enemy gets us to settle for the easy, sure thing instead of the more challenging and difficult, which would stretch and grow us.

- Insensitivity: This enemy deafens us to human needs and feelings that our inner spirit knows are worth understanding and responding to through our actions.

- Fragile ego: This enemy wants us to believe failure is never of our own making, never a result of our doing what we are unfit to do even though our inner spirit tries to get us to face the truth.

- Self-deception: This enemy offers us pleasant-sounding excuses that get us off the hook when we don't accept responsibility for our actions. If we begin to question our motives, as shameful as those motives are, this enemy gives us pleasant-sounding excuses. It lets us believe things we want to believe, even though we know they are not really true.

- Other people's expectations: This enemy causes us to listen to what others think we should be or do instead of what our hearts say to us.

By defeating these enemies, your inner voice can become a useful source of guidance to the many questions we all struggle with every day: What should I do with my life? How ought I to express my uniqueness? Dare I be creative? And in what ways? Which path ought I to take?

Listening to your inner voice will enable you to see deeply into what takes place around yourself and realize how you and others act and choose. It will help you decide whether you ought or ought not to act as you do. It will allow you to take strength and wisdom from powers within yourself and from powers beyond yourself. It will guide you to become a more likeable, attractive, capable person.

CHAPTER 4

Put People First

Treat all people as persons, not as things

Perhaps the most significant reality that we live with day to day is the fact we exist in a world with other people in it. It is unfathomable that anyone could have a meaningful life were it not for the existence of others. The quality of our earthly experience is determined largely, if not almost entirely, by the nature of our relationships with others. They are the source of our greatest joys and our greatest sorrows. Nearly all of our ethical duties exist because we live alongside others. While humans have demonstrated real genius in how to create and make things, the record of their performance in living amicably with each other leaves much to be desired. Our need for guiding principles for how to treat others is great. The challenge is to know how to live well without harming others—how to avoid disputes or settle them before conflict becomes destructive. We would be well served by guidance for living in ways that elevate our own lives and the lives of others. Clearly our quality of life is determined by how we treat ourselves and each other.

A key to understanding the ethical obligations that people owe themselves and others lies in recognizing the differences that set humans apart from objects and other life forms. While most of us believe that as humans we have no ethical obligations to rocks or trees, perhaps some to toads, but clearly many to other human beings—particularly to those with whom we share life's most intimate treasures— we aren't all that clear as to "why?" The answer to the "why?" question lies in comprehending the qualitative differences between humans and other forms of life.

Humans are not the strongest creatures, nor the swiftest, nor the best adapted for living in nature's elements. Other species are far better suited to their natural surroundings. Some have brains enabling them to communicate and reason, albeit crudely. Even the casual observer knows that all living things that have a brain know what they want and how to get it. What's most extraordinary about humans—what sets us apart—is our capacity to examine our own behavior and render moral judgments on it. We can choose what we think about and what we do. We can influence what we want and how we go about getting those wants satisfied. And, we have the capacity to examine ourselves and say "yes" or "no" to our appetites. Every decent life is derived from the exercise of moral capacities. The glory of a human lies in the ability to choose not to satisfy an unwholesome appetite, and to choose to give up some things to achieve other things of greater worth.

Nearly every advance in the human condition can be traced to the thoughtful exercise of moral reason and thoughtful choices that place the highest value on human life. We cannot say that our world is better off now, either materially or culturally or morally, than it was 100 centuries ago, because of the contributions made to it by rocks or plants or wild animals. Rocks, plants, and wild animals have not changed in the past 10,000 years. Some species of plants and animals that once lived may be extinct now, some natural resources may have been depleted, but all that remain are much the same as they have been for many centuries. What we can say is that our world is vastly different today than it was centuries ago because of the thoughts and actions of humans. The point that should capture our consideration here is that the human condition is not static. It can improve or worsen because of what people value, think, and do. Many believe that having the capacity for moral reasoning obligates humans to exercise it and to work for the betterment of everyone, themselves included.

It is widely accepted that each human is qualitatively different. Each one is a locus of individual desire and aspiration, with potentialities for creativity and self-controlled action. Each human is capable of unique contributions. Whereas one specimen of palm tree or zebra muscle or walrus is essentially indistinguishable from other palm trees or zebra muscles or walruses of the same species—each one performs the same functions in the ecological system as do the others—the same cannot be said of humans. This is because human expression ranges far beyond physical dimensions. It involves the creative element that produces progress, the compassion element that eases life's tragedies, the daring element that makes outcomes succeed. And each person expresses creativity, compassion, and daring in unique ways.

For centuries the best minds of our race have struggled with the question of how humans ought to be treated, and they have arrived at strikingly similar conclusions. Although stated in slightly different ways, they are agreed on the essential idea: Things are to be used in the service of humans; humans should never be used in the service of things. We can state this idea as a maxim: Treat others as people, not as things. Things may be used as implements because they have no self-consciousness, and the element of pain (physical or psychological) is not present. Things may be used to elevate, or serve, the betterment of something of infinitely more worth, humans. I can therefore, in good conscience, cut trees to build a house for myself or another person, but it is an outrage to harm a person in order to build a structure. The good life begins to appear when we treat others as ends, not as means to our ends. This is the basis of civilized living for all peoples. If humans held themselves to a lesser standard they could easily condone things like slavery, child labor, abuse, and torture. The strong would be able to prey on the weak. Strength and force would determine whether one were an exploiter or a victim.

The Duty to Prevent Mistreatment of Others

How one treats others is a fair measure of a person's character. This is particularly true when it comes to how those at the top of an organization treat those at the lowest levels. Even the simplest incident can tell us a great deal about a person. Many years ago a man named Paul Galvin, of Chicago, had an idea. It was a very good idea and he made it work. Paul was aware of two relatively young and rapidly growing products at the time—the automobile and the radio. And he saw a possibility of how to use them jointly. What if one were to make a radio that could operate in an automobile? It was more than a wild dream. Paul Galvin went to work on his idea and he made it work. And his company, Motorola, prospered because of it. But there is another fascinating dimension to Paul Galvin, and I want to tell you about it.

Paul also had very definite ideas on how those who built his radios and other products should be treated. The following illustrates what I mean. One day while Paul was visiting one of his plants he noticed a group of women working on a production line. That wasn't so unusual, but these women were bundled up in overcoats trying to keep out the cold. Paul asked the shop foreman, "why?" The answer: because they were running production on a single line and the remainder of the shop was idle, they were cutting costs by conserving fuel and heat.

Paul Galvin reacted sternly: "I don't care if there is one woman working, or ten, or one hundred. You treat them all alike and don't save money by abusing anyone." There it is. That's how he felt. Paul was the kind of human being who treated everyone with great respect (Petrakis, 1965).

As Paul Galvin's example shows us, genuine character is revealed by authentic concern for others. People are treated right because of the belief they should be treated right, not because of how it might benefit an employer. This starts with a flat-out refusal to not allow the mistreatment of anyone. Of course, the competitive pressures of business tend to work against this ideal. How easy it is to become so concerned with the bottom line that one begins to neglect those who work to make profitable results possible in the first place. Let me tell you about an incident that demonstrates how another person rose above these pressures.

Colgate-Palmolive's board chairman and CEO, Reuben Mark, told me about an incident some time ago that occurred when he visited a company plant in Argentina. He had traveled there to discuss business growth with the local management. Capital additions and plant expansion were the main topics on their agenda. After their meetings, Reuben toured the facility. When he walked through the employee locker rooms, he was outraged by what he saw. The change areas were filthy, so terrible no one would even want to go inside. He was not about to allow these conditions to exist in a Colgate Company plant. Reuben demanded that the change areas be renovated immediately. He would not rest easy until he knew the matter had been handled completely. So, he told the local management to telex him when they got the locker rooms fixed. That's integrity, holding principles intact against the temptation to look out for what can be easily gotten by mistreating others.

There is another dimension to integrity in relationships that's worth mentioning. Integrity also includes actively looking for the possibility of employee mistreatment before it ever happens. It means managing in ways that cause everyone to hold a high regard for others. Here is an illustration: Many years ago, several UPS managers were reviewing building plans for a sorting facility to be located in the basement of one of the company's buildings. Company founder and CEO, Jim Casey, was present. After listening to the discussion for a while Casey asked a question. "What about the ventilation for the people who will be working down there?" His first concern was for his employees. Knowing what their boss was like, these managers had a ready answer—ventilation would be provided.

Seek the Welfare of Others, Impartially, as You Do Your Own

Beyond the basic prohibition against mistreating others, integrity involves going much further. In his much-acclaimed volume, *Groundwork of the Metaphysics of Morals* (1785), Immanuel Kant (1724–1804) identified his famous categorical imperative, from which all moral commands are derived. He stated this in three progressive versions, the second of which is this:

> "So act that thou doest treat every man, whether in thine own person or that of another, as always an end withal, and never as a means."

In simple terms, Kant's imperative means this: Make no person a pawn in your game of life. Clearly, we would not like to be used by others for their greedy purposes, and neither would anyone else. Every normal, well-adjusted person seeks his or her own welfare. We want to live healthy, fulfilled, productive lives free of pain and privation. But there is more to this than most people see on the surface. We are responsible for ourselves, to make something of ourselves, to be useful and live a meaningful existence. And, in addition to not mistreating others, we are also obliged to seek the same good life, the same welfare for others that we seek for ourselves. This expresses the fundamental basis for our Western concept of justice, the impartial treatment of all people. This is not altruism, which places the welfare of others ahead of self. I do not owe others more than I owe myself. But I do not owe them any less either. This concept of even-handed treatment means that I should be impartial, that I must not make a distinction between my welfare and the welfare of my neighbor.

Whirlpool's first CEO, Elisha Gray II, had a method for being totally honest when it came to considering others whenever he contemplated a decision. "In the course of making any business decision," said Gray, "I find it useful to ask myself, 'How would I feel if I were at the other end of this deal?' On numerous occasions I did not like the answer I got and that was generally enough to change my course of action" (from a Whirlpool Corp. pamphlet). Most readers are well familiar with this idea. They know it as the Golden Rule: Treat others as you would want to be treated. The ancient Israelites had a similar commandment: Thou shalt love thy neighbor as thyself.

Southwest Airline's former CEO, Herb Kelleher, espoused this philosophy toward his employees: "We could have furloughed [our employees] at various times and been more profitable, but I always thought that was short-sighted. You want to show your people that you value them and you're not going to hurt them to get a little more money in the short term" (Brooker, 2001).

An acquaintance of mine named Phil Hampton, who was vice chairman of Bankers Trust of New York at the time of this incident, once told me about a situation his firm went through where he had to decide between added profit and the well-being of employees. It caused Bankers Trust to stand up and meet what they considered an implied obligation to those who had been loyal employees for many years. Bankers Trust had put a small part of its business on the market, and several bids were received for the bank branches they wanted to sell. Naturally, Phil was most interested in the best offer. In fact he had a fiduciary responsibility to his company's stockholders to obtain the best price he could get. So, he proceeded to enter into negotiations on the final terms of the sale. Now, Bankers Trust stipulated that it was not just selling an asset it was selling a business, complete with loyal employees. Phil made it clear from the start that Bankers Trust expected the purchaser to guarantee their employees the pensions they had earned. Bankers Trust also stipulated that the sale was contingent on the buyer's agreement to keep all current employees on the payroll for at least one year.

When the top bidder's proposal came in and Phil's team examined it, they found it was vague regarding these stipulations. Phil expressed his concern and the prospective buyer agreed to come back with another offer, one that addressed the employee issues. They told Phil, "We may have to offer you less for this business." Phil said, "Fine. The deal is negotiable."

But the second proposal was still vague. And so, after thinking it over, Phil and his team came to the conclusion that this prospective buyer really had no intention of treating the Bankers Trust employees involved fairly. So, Phil broke off the negotiations. Eventually Bankers Trust sold the branches to another buyer, accepting $5 million less than what they could have received from the first.

Phil told me later, "We put profit maximization behind the welfare of the people who had been long-time, loyal employees." That seemed to me to be a supreme example of following through with an implied commitment even though the only thing to be gained from it was the knowledge that the honorable thing had been done, despite the loss of profit.

Respect Feelings and Listen to Concerns

The board chairman of a major paper company once told me that he believed any problem is important to him if it is important to one of his company's employees. His is an excellent standard to emulate. This board chairman ran his organization on the principle of keeping his board of directors sensitive to issues that bother company employees. Because of this concern, things that ordinarily would not have received top management's attention came out into the open and were dealt with positively. And because of it, employee dedication and performance were extraordinary.

The chairman and his board of directors worked hard and with sincerity to uncover what troubled their employees. What they learned was eye opening. They found problems that were important to employees, not thought at first to be important to themselves. The truth is that by taking this level of interest, the chairman and his board of directors learned much more about what was on the minds of their employees than they could have possibly imagined. And it was through dealing with these matters above board and straightforwardly that they came to earn employee respect and loyalty. This is how they did it.

At brown bag lunches held every other month, employees and the company's directors discussed concerns. At one of these meetings a woman who worked in a clerical capacity started to speak but hesitated. "This is dumb," she said. "No, we want to hear," replied the directors.

What bothered her was the location of a file cabinet. She wanted it moved but never felt she should ask. It may have appeared to be a little thing to the directors but just think about what it was to the woman? Now what do you suppose that woman thinks about those directors every time she looks at that file cabinet sitting in a different spot? What is elevated in one life gets magnified in the lives of ten thousand more lives because of the ways positive attitudes spread to others.

At a paper mill in Michigan, employees revealed another irritation during one of these lunch meetings. A bridge connected the main parking lot to the plant. Next to the plant were just a few parking spaces where the managers parked. Employees had to park in the main lot and walk over the bridge to the plant, whereas the managers could drive right up to the building. They told the management, "Look, you drive, we walk. Yet we get here a lot earlier than you do." Managers never realized this had been bothering employees. The situation was changed. Parking was immediately put on a first-come basis. Again, do you think these employees now feel differently about their management, now that they don't have to walk past empty parking spaces close to the plant, marked with "Reserved for Management" signs, in inclement weather?

It is widely understood that a receptive ear hears much, provided employees feel comfortable voicing their thoughts and feelings. The trick is to develop a high enough level of comfort to get people to speak up. The first step is to create confidence in the minds of people. There are two requirements: Sincerity and action. Act with sincerity, and do something about what you hear. Sincere listening is strong evidence of genuine concern for employees.

One of the finest CEOs I ever met, Lewis Lehr of 3M, once told me something. He said, "If I don't understand what employees think is right, then just maybe I don't know what is right myself. In other words, they just might see something that I am missing. It is possible that they might see something that's not right that I do not see at all." Therefore, he told me that he tries to be more open minded. And by sincerely trying to understand their point of view, they tell him things he would otherwise never learn about. And, he pays attention to what his employees have to say.

This leader was an excellent listener, because he heard more than just his employees' words. He saw directly into their hearts and understood how they felt as well. His example demonstrates an important standard for effective understanding: listen for more than just words—try to sense how people feel inside.

Lewis Lehr paid attention to the organization chart; he was mindful of the chain of command. He didn't want to undermine anyone's authority. Nonetheless, he had many discussions with people who held positions anywhere in the organization. He had what's known as an open-door policy and it was effective in getting deep-seated problems out into the open, where they could be dealt with straightforwardly. Here's an illustration.

At 7:00 o'clock one morning Lehr received a telephone call at home from a group of employees. They must have been pretty mad to call him at that hour. And, indeed, these factory workers were plenty unhappy with what was going on where they worked. Lehr was a welcoming listener. They wanted to see him, Could they? "Fine," he said, "Do you want to meet me for breakfast at a restaurant we all know or do you want to come to my office?" They wanted to come to his office, which they did.

At his office that morning five factory employees told him what they thought was wrong where they worked. And Lehr got into it and learned a little more about the matter. The reason these five employees felt they could come to him was because he had earlier befriended an employee in their factory—an elevator operator who had a health problem. She had a weight and back problem and someone was trying to put her back in a line operation job that she couldn't physically handle. Mr. Lehr learned about that and made a few suggestions and the woman stayed on as an elevator operator. Word of that incident passed among the employees. Trust developed. If employees thought they had a problem, they knew they could talk to Mr. Lehr about it. And they did. The problem that the five employees told him about was corrected, a situation that would have festered and led to unpleasant consequences had it not been cleared up.

Make Work Meaningful—Show that It Matters

Several years ago Charlie Moritz, who was board chairman of Dun & Bradstreet at the time, held a question-and-answer session with employees after the group had met for breakfast. There was a young man at this gathering who worked in the computer room of one of the company's divisions, and he seemed to be scared to death to ask his question. He would put up his hand and then he'd pull it down. But finally he got up enough courage to ask his question. He started slowly and cautiously, telling first about his work attendance. Indeed, he had a good record. He also mentioned how hard he and others worked to produce quality results.

Finally, the young man got around to the real reason for his speaking up in the first place. He said, "My question is this: Where does my work go, and is it important to anybody?" Charlie was taken aback by this totally honest question. He thought to himself, "What an incredibly lonely, horrible existence—to be working and not know where one's work goes and whether it is of value to anybody." Moritz launched into his answer, starting with the statement, "Everyone is entitled to meaning in their lives, and management has an obligation to provide that within the work environment." He followed this talk up with actions aimed at getting every manager and supervisor to show employees that what they did at work mattered.

I think this story reveals an important lesson: it is deceptively easy to forget that behind the many abstractions in business—production reports, sales figures, profit and loss statements, and the like—there are human beings. Integrity involves far more than just not mistreating others. It also includes the belief that human beings are entitled to more than just a paycheck and benefits. They ought as well receive recognition and derive a sense of worth and dignity from doing their work.

Respect Others by Showing Recognition

One of the most important things to know about human beings is their need for recognition. We all want to feel we are needed, that we are useful, that what we do counts for something. We all want to feel significant. Yet many a life is rarely touched by the uplifting influence of recognition. As a result, many fine men and women never fully blossom into what they might otherwise become. It cannot be urged too forcefully that people ought to recognize each other and that managers in particular ought to recognize their employees. There are two important aspects of recognition to keep in mind. The first is to recognize people for their abilities by putting them to work on challenging assignments. And the second is to recognize people for their accomplishments, for the good things they have done, by the simple act of praise.

People have a need to be needed. The first way we can show recognition is by putting people to work. I recall hearing a story told by George Albee, a former president of the American Psychological Association. It was about a man who was a high-powered, successful business executive. This man ran, almost single-handedly, an important operation for his company that nobody else fully understood. When this man reached the age of sixty-four, top management decided they had better get a replacement ready to assume his job when he retired. They brought in a bright young man who apprenticed under the old master, learning the complexities of his function. The year passed by quickly, and on his sixty-fifth birthday and against his objections, the man was moved out to pasture. He didn't want to leave. In fact, he protested but the company had rules. So, he was forced out, retired.

A few months after his retirement, a dramatic change overcame the man. He began to withdraw from his family and friends, because he felt useless. He seemed to be losing his zest for living, and he was losing it fast. In less than a year of his retirement this once lively, productive businessman was hospitalized, diagnosed as suffering from senile psychosis. Friends and family tried to cheer him up but he didn't respond to their visits. His condition worsened further.

After a while, those who knew him gave up trying to lift him out of his state of decline. They stopped visiting him. He had become a vegetable.

Within a couple of years, the young man who had taken over the older man's job died tragically. Now, the company faced a problem. No one was able to perform this important function. What were they to do? A decision was made to try to approach the old man and see if he could pull himself together and come back to his old job. Several of his former co-workers went to the hospital to talk to him. After several hours of trying to get through to him a sparkle entered his eyes. The idea of returning to his old job began to sink in and he responded with new life. Within a few days, this man who had become little more than a vegetable was back at work, functioning as he had before retirement.

Again, another young man was brought in as his understudy. And within a few years after that, the older man was re-retired. Within a year he re-entered the hospital, never to leave.

There is a second way we show recognition, and people love it. It is by the simple act of saying "thank you" for a job well done. This shows that one's work matters, that it is valued. Many years ago, when I worked for the Anaconda Company, I taught this important idea to our mining foremen. One of them, a man by the name of Claude Huber, took this lesson to heart and used it the first chance he got. Claude worked in one of Anaconda's underground copper mines in Butte, Montana.

At quitting time one day, Claude noticed the especially fine job of timbering one of his men had done, shoring up a newly cut shaft. So, Claude took the time to inspect it, commenting favorably about what he observed. The old man who had spent all day doing this job appeared pleased at first. But then something strange and unexpected happened. He began to get emotional and he teared up. He said to Claude, "That's the first time anyone has ever told me that. Nobody even cared before."

What a horrible thing it must be to feel that what you do doesn't matter. But what an incredibly wonderful feeling it must be to realize that it really does matter and that others notice. I know that this experience taught Claude an important lesson, because he said so to me. I also know it did a great deal to uplift the spirits and motivation of that man, who did such a fine job that day. And I know he performed many other jobs in excellent fashion from that day since.

Defeat Hatred with a Positive Spirit of Goodwill

It is easy to agree with the idea that people ought not to harm others. While this ideal sits well with our intellect, it does not always dominate our feelings and control our actions. Consider the man who wanted to be the one selected to sell a new line of adhesives his company manufactured. He knew he could use his knowledge of chemistry to convince buyers of the product's superior qualities. But he was more of a "techie" than he was a smooth-talking salesman and higher-ups in his organization knew this. When they selected his friend for his plum position, the man felt bad. And the more he thought about missing out on getting what he wanted, the more this man grew angry.

At first he was only angry at those who made the selection decision. But after a time his anger enlarged its reach to include his friend, who got the job that he wanted. As this man's anger festered inside, he began to feel that he had been cheated, that he deserved the job. He began hating his boss, and the bosses above, and his company for ignoring his abilities. But all this happened many years ago and it should have been long forgotten. Indeed, this man would have felt better about himself had he been able to put it all behind him. But he just wouldn't do that. He couldn't. He held on to his resentments, particularly those toward the man who got the job he wanted. After a while the man who didn't get the job began to view the other man as his arch rival. He became jealous, and his jealousy brought its twin brother, vindictiveness, into the picture. And so, now every chance this man gets he tries to destroy his rival. Nothing in this world warps a person's judgment quite like hatred. Once a person allows himself to hate, he can neither think nor see straight, nor listen without distortion. Hatred can start small and grow out of control inside a person in a way that no other emotion can. And it makes the one who holds it impervious to reason and the rules of common decency. Whenever hatred toward a person gets going, it robs those in its grip of their reason. They lose all sense of proportion.

Many people can become so preoccupied with their own feelings that they are unable to consider the feelings of anyone else. Whenever this happens, the situation is ripe for someone to get hurt. Meanness can arise and words can be spoken aimed at damaging another person's reputation. Rumors get passed around, and the motives behind them have a way of leading to mean and hurtful actions. More rumors circulate; the truth gets twisted and those passing the rumors turn cruel. Worse yet, these people justify their actions with high-minded reasons; all the while they make up stories against their enemy and do whatever mean, hurtful thing they can imagine to rid this unwanted person from their organization and send him on his way, wounded and with a ruined reputation.

While it is true that we have no control over our hearts in terms of to whom they respond either favorably or unfavorably—we really cannot decide who we will or will not fall in love with—it is also true that we can conquer hatred and indifference with goodwill. At one time or another, each of us will find ourselves liking and having favorable reactions to some of the people we encounter and experiencing the opposite sorts of reactions toward others. This is human. But the decisive element that indicates depth of character in anyone is goodwill, an honestly felt desire for the well-being of everyone. For without goodwill, hatred and all the forms of unpleasantness and mean, uncivil acts it stirs up can easily penetrate mind and heart. The only escape we have from hatred is being big minded ourselves. The secret lies in genuinely wanting the other person to experience a good life. Say to yourself, "I wish good things for this other person, no matter how despicable I might feel that person is. If I can do this, then I have a good chance of saving myself from the clutches of hatred and all the destruction it will surely bring upon me."

Treat Others Right

Let's summarize the main points of this chapter:

1. Don't tolerate the mistreatment of others. Work to prevent it in the first place and take corrective actions whenever you spot it.
2. Seek the welfare of others just as you do your own.
3. Respect other people's feelings. Listen to them. Act on them.
4. Make work meaningful. Show people that their work matters.
5. Recognize work that has been performed well.
6. Hold a spirit of goodwill toward everyone.

CHAPTER 5

Pass the Utmost Test

Choose the best thing over good things

People everywhere are making themselves miserable trying to possess things that are mutually exclusive, and they always fail. Although they know it's impossible for a body to occupy two places at the same time physically, their actions demonstrate an unwillingness to accept what amounts to be the same basic idea: one cannot have two things that preclude each other. I can choose to lie to get what I want from others but I cannot be secure in holding on to their trust. I can be a gossip and act the part of a busybody but I cannot long enjoy a reputation for discretion and minding my own business. I can choose to brag about my abilities and accomplishments but I cannot escape being labeled egotistical and an insufferable bore. I must choose.

When we observe what's going on around us, it is plainly evident that people are choosing continuously. They continuously choose to be where they are now instead of being other places; they continuously choose to pursue what they are doing now instead of doing other things. No one escapes these kinds of decisions. We are making them all the time, every moment. The basic difficulty many people get themselves into is being diverted from things of greater value by things of lesser value, by saying yes to the demands coming from second-rate matters that keep them from pursuing what's most meaningful. A sure test of character involves the ability to distinguish the best from the second-rate. And it also involves the wisdom and strength of will to subordinate those pursuits of lesser worth to those of supreme importance. This is the Utmost Test and everyone faces it: whether we put the best ahead of the good.

Don't Allow the Second-Rate to Crowd Out the First-Rate

Last week I had to fly across country to attend a meeting. It was a three-hour flight and I planned to use the time to catch up on some reading. But as it turned out, I didn't, and for that I fault myself for not putting first things first—myself. Regardless, I sat next to two people who were engaged in a lively conversation about office politics. I'm sure they worked together.

I admit it. I eavesdropped on their conversation—and here, again, I must admit another failure, listening to gossip. But what I heard made me realize something terribly important. Contempt is a terrible and corrosive emotion. These two people were negative and highly cynical. For every person they mentioned, they had a criticism. From what they said, I concluded that nothing suited them. Every person in their organization, they believed, had the lowest of motives. They thought that higher-ups where they worked knew nothing, that underlings were lazy and incompetent, and that those at their level were self-serving and underhanded. From what I could gather, the only two people in their organization who had any insight and capability were themselves. I even wondered what each might have to say about the other, were they apart and talking to someone else.

I thought to myself how utterly petty and wasteful, even down-right harmful, their conversation was. What a waste of time. I felt a little ashamed of myself for listening to them. Later that day I felt even more ashamed of myself for enjoying what I heard. Here I was, listening to two strangers gossip, and in doing so, my behavior was little different from theirs. I, too, was prone to being just as cynical, just as ready to delight in gossip, and just as small-minded as they were acting.

Millions of conversations like the one I overheard on the airplane are going on right now around the globe. These kinds of conversations are seductive. Perhaps it's our desire to feel good about ourselves that leads us to talk ill of others. But that's not our concern here. Instead, let's examine an important way in which small-minded gossip prevents us from fully becoming the persons we might be.

The next time you drive out into the countryside, where power transmission lines run alongside the road, try tuning your car's radio to an AM station. Chances are good that you won't be able to hear what these AM stations are broadcasting because of the static created by the electricity in the power lines overhead. The static will be so unbearable that you'll either turn your radio off or change to an FM station. If only we would react to gossip and cynical conversations like we do when the noise of static blares from our car's radio. But that's not the way gossip and cynical conversations sound to our ears. Unlike the static that prevents our car radios from turning broadcast signals into the music and talk that we want to hear, gossip is seductive. It arrives in the alluring disguise of appealing "music"— at least it's a different form of "music." I think gossip is appealing, because it so often makes us feel slightly superior to others. This is among the most common forms of bad crowding out good that I can think of. We allow gossip to tune out our positive thoughts, and it holds our attention on second-rate matters when we could be tending to first-rate ones. To be fully successful in our lives we must completely subordinate second-rate desires to those that are first-rate. This unlearned truth has cost many people severely.

Rise Above the Paralysis of Indecision

Living an effective life, one that is above confusion and trouble, demands a persistent pattern of wise choices. The difficulty most people face is (1) deciding which things they prize most highly and then (2) giving up other things they also want and find pleasing but that preclude having the first. But for many people, perhaps most people, there is usually some aspect of their life where they cannot seem to come to a firm decision, where they keep going back and forth from one thing they want at the time to another thing they also want, and then back again to the first. This unsettled pattern of first choosing one thing and then another and then back to the first thing again, like having one foot in a boat and the other foot on a dock, can prove disastrous. It adversely affects one's mental state and it invariably leaves the person an emotional wreck and unsatisfied, because neither aim is fully achieved.

Upon graduation from a teachers' college in his native Italy, Luciano Pavarotti asked his father, "Shall I be a teacher or a singer?"

"Luciano," his father replied, "if you try to sit on two chairs you will fall between them. For life you must choose one chair." The tenor superstar chose one. After 7 years of difficult study and frustration, he made his first professional appearance. Whatever we choose, we do our best when we give ourselves to it. Commitment, that's the key. Choose one chair.

In many realms of life it is foolish to think one can "have it both ways." Between a life of loose living and a secure marriage there can be no compromise. I can choose to give in to my desires and gorge myself with rich foods and fine wines, as does a glutton. But if I want good health, then I must subordinate the desires of my palate to habits that promote good health. If I try doing both, I will end up only somewhat overweight and in slightly poor health but not in good health. If I have the raw talent and want to become a competitive collegiate swimmer, I must choose to spend time training instead of hanging out with friends and listening to music. If I try both, I may or may not make the swim team but I will certainly never be a great swimmer. One must choose. A mark of integrity is the willingness to admit and then to subordinate what is good to what is best.

While it's true that our heart's true desires are made evident by the patterns of our choices, it is also sometimes true that our desires have difficulty growing enough inside our hearts to register clearly in our minds. People who find themselves in this predicament wander from one thing that they think they want at one time to another thing they feel they want later on, and then, after that, to something else. Like a child with 50 cents who is standing in a candy store and is unable to decide, they agonize over their confusion.

Consider a situation in which many good people find themselves today. One woman captured the essence of this particular difficulty when she explained her confusion. "I never got a chance to go beyond high school. I married young and had my children early in life. After they left the nest, I looked for ways to earn extra money. My husband's job doesn't pay very well and sometimes he's out of work. I work part time when I can but employers want people they can count on regularly. A few years ago I took bookkeeping classes at our local college. I like bookkeeping. I do it on the side when I can. But I haven't had a chance to pursue it full time. Actually, I have a dream of starting my own business as a book-keeper. My biggest problem is time. There isn't enough of it. My kids need me to babysit for them so they can go to work. I have a mother who's having trouble getting around and she needs me to drive her to the grocery store and her doctor's office. My husband is constantly asking me to do things for him—I wish he were more independent. I don't mind doing things for others. It makes me feel needed. But still, it seems that all I do is to help out others. I don't have time to do what I'd really like to do. And that is to start my own business."

This woman is torn between doing things for others and doing what she wants with her own life. Her predicament is one of the most widespread diffi-culties that caring people in our busy world face. Like a rope used in a tug of war, she is being pulled at from two different directions. Family demands pull at her one way. Her desire to do what she wants with her own life pulls at her the other way. No one can move in two directions at the same time. No one can live peaceably with themselves under the stress of competing demands. She feels boxed in, helpless to decide how she will live her life.

Her interior war of feelings, pulling at her from opposite directions, immo-bilizes her to choose. Feelings of guilt and regret render her helpless. It is a painful and unhappy experience, and it ruins lives. She is confused and unhappy. If she chooses to pursue her dream of a small business, then family demands go to work on her mind and heart by making her feel guilty. But, if she chooses to spend her time doing nice things to please others, then feelings of regret and a lack of fulfillment burden her mind and heart.

The war of feelings not only immobilizes a person, it also renders them inef-fective and over time, worse yet, incapable of ever acting wholeheartedly in doing anything. But for now, this woman still has a chance. She first needs to believe that she has the power to free herself from this state of helplessness and reclaim her freedom to choose for herself. But she needs to proceed cautiously. The first step is to examine her own feelings and understand the realities of her predicament. She needs to take a long, hard look at herself, her drives, and her wants.

Part of the tension she experiences could be coming from an excessive need to feel needed. To be sure many people want to feel needed. Practically everyone wants to experience the feeling of appreciation. Few things in life run deeper than that. But one can focus too much on satisfying this desire. Over concern for appreciation can deafen one to other, legitimate desires that are good for us, too, maybe even better for us. What makes the desire for appreciation deceptively harmful is the fact that the ways in which most people try to earn appreciation involve doing good things. And they erroneously conclude that no possible harm can come from doing good things.

It's possible to consider this woman's desire to do good deeds from another angle. She watches her grandchildren so her own children can go to work. Maybe she thinks her grown children need an income more than she needs one herself. But could it also be possible that her children are really taking advantage of her goodness? It might well be that they employ a terrible, manipulative ploy called guilt, and they use it to their advantage to get her to do what they want. A well-adjusted person turns a deaf ear to this manipulative ploy. Emotionally stable people recognize that this form of guilt, the kind used by others to get their way, is fundamentally different than the kind of guilt our conscience causes us to feel when we do wrong.

This woman would not be the person she is were she not so concerned about others. But she is also a woman who wants to start her own business. She needs to realize that she was given a life to live and living responsibly involves exercising her abilities to think and choose and act. Indeed, responsible living involves making choices. It is true that one cannot please everyone. It is also true that one cannot do all things at the same time. You may choose to spend the later part of an afternoon resolving a complaint from an important customer or attending your child's softball game. But you cannot do both, even though both are important to you and you would like to do both. She needs to accept the fact that the more time she gives to one demand, the less time will she be able to devote to the other demand. She cannot pursue her own dreams and do all the things that her family members demand of her. She has to choose. There is no middle ground.

This woman needs to honestly face up to the fact that she has the power to choose. As it is now, guilt is doing its best to confuse and immobilize her, and it is causing great harm to her peace of mind. This woman needs to affirm her power to choose, to take control of her life. If there are compromises to be made, she needs to realize that she has the power to make them. This woman will experience a sense of inner peace when she accepts the fact that by pursuing her own goals, she will not be able to do all she would like to do for others. And, that by doing for others, she will not be able to do all she wants for herself. She will learn that she need not feel ashamed for wanting to become self-sufficient and independent, that she is not being selfish or unlovely because she asserts her independence.

When this woman faces her struggle squarely and seizes control of her own life by making her own decisions, she will experience a sense of satisfaction that her courage to choose is stronger than her feelings of guilt and regret. Once she finds the right answer for herself, the best thing she can do is to act on it and not look back or second-guess herself. If she does, she will invite back the devilish forces of confusion, which are ever ready to retake control and make her helpless and miserable once again.

Only when we accept the reality that we cannot possess mutually exclusive things and that having one at the cost of the other is better than having neither, accompanied by the agony of indecision, will we be in a position to freely exercise our power of choice. Squandering or surrendering the power of choice to other forces diminishes one's dignity, well-being, and effectiveness.

Develop a Sense of Proportion and Be Truthful

Without a good sense of proportion, people encounter all kinds of difficulties. They limit their achievements, doing small things while big ones go undone. They fret and stew over trivial matters while real emergencies go unattended. They allow their concern for what is second-rate to crowd out their concern for the first-rate. And then, to save themselves from embarrassment and shame, they make up excuses to justify their poor decisions. This phenomenon appears in every way imaginable:

- A capable employee fails to meet a deadline. The project she was assigned required more time than she anticipated it would, but she spent a weekend with friends anyway, instead of finishing her work.
- A supervisor of mechanics cannot keep his hands off the work to be done. His subordinates stand back as he takes over. He tells himself that he is helping them do difficult portions of their jobs, which he's much better at performing than they are.
- A section head allows a bad piece of work to move forward through the manufacturing process because he feels too busy with other worries to do anything about it.

- A newly hired staff worker feels that the way to move ahead is to get noticed. She performs a particular piece of work quite well and then spends the better part of the next several days trying to win recognition from higher-ups.

These are not evil people doing bad things; they are good people doing dumb things. Their mistake is giving their best energy to less important matters when they could be performing more important ones. They concentrate on good things when they could be focusing on the best things. They do not have a good sense of proportion, because they are not honest about what is most important. Honesty enables one to focus on the main things to be accomplished and not the trifling details, which are easy or fun or provide greater enjoyment at the time. It is one thing to choose work that is right for oneself. It is another thing to give second-rate concerns too high a priority, at the expense of not doing the most important things, because the lesser things are easier and more convenient. All too often we find ourselves sliding along the unthinking groove of habit, getting by with the least amount of effort. When we do this, we rob our employer and we shortchange ourselves.

Of all the reasons why people get distracted by the trivial and fail to concentrate on the most important, none is commoner than concern for self. Peer into the heart of any person, and one of the most limiting weaknesses to be found there is overconcern for self—its appetite for praise, its sense of importance, its desire for things pleasurable, its narrowness of concern, its fear of looking the fool, its quickness to anger. The list is long, and the road to misery and failure is paved with its many possibilities.

The persistent desires of self have a way of crowding the best things out of our thoughts. But its mischief doesn't stop there. The self-comes-first mentality also distorts and twists the truth about things—especially ourselves and our actions. This mind set is known for turning one's likes into wants, and then these wants into deserves, and then these deserves into necessities, must-haves, and entitlements. These desires twist people's reasoning, giving them plausible excuses to use in defending their choices.

The woman who spent her weekend having fun with friends instead of completing an important assignment, defends her actions by saying she was not hired to work weekends, that the project can wait and that, besides, she needs the time off to renew her energy level. The mechanic who cannot keep his hands off his underling's work covers up his dislike for supervisory duties by doing what he most likes. He allows his preference for hands-on tasks, instead of showing others how to perform work, to give him a reason to feel that he's doing his organization a service. The section head who allows bad work to slip by because he is more concerned with easier matters that he can handle routinely excuses his inaction by saying he was "just too busy." And, finally, the newly hired staff worker who did perform well mistakenly believes that getting ahead means getting noticed and that if others don't see what she did, then she must tell them about it. In so many ways the self is at the center of our wanting something that is of little consequence. By giving in to it, we hold ourselves back from extraordinary performance.

Security or Challenge and Adventure? You Cannot Have Both. You Must Choose

There are literally millions of capable men and women in the world marking time, going nowhere because they are frozen by the fear of trying something different. Their thoughts scan the possibilities of challenge and opportunity and weigh these against the predictability of guaranteed rewards. Then fear and insecurity whisper in their ears that they ought not chance looking bad, losing face, or risking failure. These people may want to try something new in their careers. They might want to escape a boring routine. They may even feel stifled and want to venture out into doing something different. But they cannot overcome their worries: "I may not like this new kind of work," they think. "My identity and self-image are wrapped up in terms of my specialty and that is too important to me to risk losing." "This untried opportunity may require talents I don't have and I could fail." At the same time, while they hold these thoughts, they are not entirely fulfilled with what they do now and secretly wish they could be doing something different.

I once met a man who faced this kind of dilemma. He told me that when he started working in construction 28 years ago, he saw operating heavy equipment as a macho thing. "You feel powerful when you operate earth-movers, bull-dozers, scrapers, scoop shovels," he told me. "It's not the weight you move. It's the technique. I was good at it." Wherever he worked, his bosses liked him because he got the work done quickly and because he did not abuse the machinery. He told me that some of the guys he worked with would do dumb things when operating machinery, thinking it was smart to take chances. Supervisors didn't like that, and they got mad when the equipment was down for repairs.

The man said that after a several years of doing this kind of work and being seen as good at it, he began to think of himself differently. He started to take pride in not just the "macho" work he did but also in how well he did it. He wasn't bashful about his abilities. He said, "There aren't that many guys who can handle machinery nearly as well as I can. It takes lots of years to get good at something, I mean really good." Recently, upper management at the construction firm where he works asked him if he'd like to train younger guys. He said that they want him to teach younger employees the techniques and methods he uses.

I asked him, "What is so bad about that? You'd get a raise in pay and have better hours."

"That's not what bothers me," he replied. "I wonder if they think I'm slowing down, not pushing the work out as well as I once did. I told them I'd have to think about it for a while. I just don't know. I mean, I have always thought of myself as an operator. I have lots of pride in that. I don't know if I could relate to these younger guys. Maybe they wouldn't listen to what I have to tell them. They don't listen very well, you know."

"Okay, then," I said, "The best choice for you is to turn down the opportunity and stick with what you know and what gives you so much satisfaction."

"Oh, I don't know about that," he said. "These young guys could benefit from my experience."

"Have you ever considered the possibility that the managers above you see something in you that you don't see in yourself?" I asked him. "Have you thought of how they might see the opportunity that you, with all your experience, present to them?"

"How so?" he asked.

"It seems to me that they need more operators like you and that if you were to pass along what you know, then others would perform their jobs better. Isn't that what upper management most wants—more first-rate operators?" I asked.

"I have thought about that," he admitted. "I'd like to do that. I suppose that the objections and worries that I mentioned earlier really are not my main concerns. If I were to be honest, completely honest, I suppose my main concern is to protect my status. I like being the best operator. I guess I jealously guard that distinction."

"So then," I said, "the real choice is between the sure thing of remaining an operator and enjoying a distinction of being good and the risk of chancing your reputation on a different assignment and improving the skills of many others?"

"Yes," he said, "That's the choice I need to make."

Among the sadder pages found in any human life are tales of missed chances, untried opportunities that could have led to success and immense satisfaction. All too often the crust forms too quickly on a human's development and the life that might have been never fully rises. Consider the technically trained person who could have done exceptionally well in sales but chooses to remain in a narrow capacity as a specialist where the routine is comfortable and the rewards predictable. We are all drawn to the warmth of the fireplace and the comfort of the easy chair where we feel secure and safe. But is safe admirable? We want what's safe and we'd like to try things with risk; we enjoy the known but are intrigued by the unknown, and we like the predictability and stability of sameness but we'd also like an element of adventure. Regardless of our likes and wants, we still must choose. We cannot possess both. We must determine what's most important and subordinate things of lesser importance to that. We must choose which way our lives should go; we must choose to do what we believe we were meant to do.

How different the history of major league baseball would be had a certain New York Yankee player remained in a position that he played exceptionally well. Suppose he said "no," that he would not move from being a pitcher (he was an excellent pitcher) to playing in the outfield and batting every game. Had George Herman Ruth continued pitching, he would still have gotten in the record books but he certainly would not have become "Babe Ruth," baseball's greatest icon.

I know of many people, and you do, too, who started out in one field and shifted to another one. In trying to do something they never did before, they met success or failure, satisfaction or dissatisfaction. Whatever they found from their experience with the new, be it delightful or disturbing, the important thing they came away with is this: a clearer, deeper understanding of themselves.

Become the Person You Are Meant to Be

It is true that many people achieve a good record when it comes to putting good things ahead of bad things, doing what's productive instead of what's unproductive, acting in constructive ways instead of destructive ways, being ethical instead of unethical. The greatest difficulty arrives whenever we must choose between the very best and the very good, between the best things and simply good things. Imagine the sales manager who does well for her firm by achieving exceptional growth in her sales territory. Her boss calls her in and tells her that upper management wants to promote her to vice president of sales. This position pays three times what she now makes, and it provides a bonus package of stock options worth millions, provided she reaches established targets. But this more responsible position will not come without great sacrifice. It will require her to be on the road six nights a week and to work on weekends. A shrewd person will examine possible ways to get what's wanted and proceed with the most expedient way of achieving those ambitions. People of integrity approach choices with a different concern. They ask themselves whether pursuing something they might want makes them the kind of persons they would most like to be.

Study the lives of our country's most successful personalities, and I think you'll see a pattern of certain traits that account for much of their success. In each life there is to be found some extraordinary quality that sets it apart. Consider the story of a man named Milton, and his lifelong passion for building something worthwhile that led to his greatest achievements and joy. Milton was a wealthy man before he reached the age of 45. His candies were such a huge success that he was able to sell his caramel business for over one million dollars in 1901. It was a fabulous sum of money, particularly then. Yes, Milton, you might say, had what practically everyone would like to have had—his health, enormous wealth, and a young, beautiful wife. So, Milton thought he'd cash in and try retirement. He and his wife set out for an extended trip around the world.

They hadn't been gone for very long when Milton's wife said to him while they were in Mexico, "I am not having such a wonderful time on this trip as I had anticipated, and I would be happy if we were returning home." Milton was thinking exactly the same thing, his mind still more on what he might have been doing in business than it was on enjoying strange countries. Milton wasn't content to sit back and enjoy his riches in the comfort of an easy chair. That wasn't his idea of enjoyment at all. He was a builder and he had something big in mind that needed building. The couple immediately cancelled their world travel plan and returned to their home in Pennsylvania. It was then that he, Milton S. Hershey, whose name has become synonymous with chocolate, decided to enter the chocolate business on a grand scale. "Not for the money that might be in it," said Milton Hershey, "but for the satisfaction of doing something that was worthwhile" (Snavely, 1935). That's it. It was the satisfaction of doing something big, something that made a difference, which accounts for Milton's incredible success.

His motives were authentic. He built a community; pioneered innovative management and personnel practices—like profit sharing and employee health and fitness; built orphanages and schools; established hospitals, libraries, and concert halls. And he brought in the finest musicians and teachers available to add to the improvement of those who lived and worked in his community—now named after him: Hershey, Pennsylvania.

The key to finding the fullest levels of success and satisfaction comes from finding what one is most suited to do. This is not easy, and those who have succeeded at it never took it lightly. Sometimes one just has to experiment, to try something out and discover how it feels, believing that the spirit that lives within each of us is a remarkably reliable judge of what's best. And so, the youngster who finds delight in caring for animals hears his inner voice telling him, "This is something that's right for you." The middle-aged person who leaves a position in manufacturing and takes a position in training and development and does well in that assignment hears an inner voice saying, "You should continue on in this field." The key is to be most guided by what our hearts tell us we were meant to be and not be misled by what we think we must have or must do to please others or to achieve status or to reach financial targets that we do not find fulfilling.

Many years ago, B. C. Forbes, who founded *Forbes* magazine and studied the most successful business leaders of his day, wrote: "The man who sets up money-making as his primary, his sole goal, who subverts everything to that end, seldom fulfills his narrow, Midas-like ambition. It is not money but the joy of achievement, the joy of creating, of developing something, that spurs on most men who become factors of first importance in the business world. Providence would seem to have ordained that the man who serves most shall reap most" (quoted in *Forbes Magazine*, July 13, 1987).

Passing the Utmost Test

1. Don't allow what's second-rate to crowd out what's first-rate.
2. Exercise your power of choice. Don't allow circumstance to paralyze you; assert your power to stand up and choose.
3. Be truthful with yourself and others when it comes to the motives behind your behaviors. Don't allow laziness and immediate desires for an easy path to lead you to doing second-rate work.
4. Decide whether you want security or challenge. Make your choice.
5. Determine what's best for you by fully understanding who you were meant to become. Learn to find "who" that person is by discovering what best resonates well with your inner spirit.

CHAPTER 6

Become a First-Rate Person

Guide your actions by civilization's highest standards, not by your immediate desires

The world is filled with millions of people who, right now, are thinking to themselves, 'I wish I hadn't done it. I knew better but I did it anyway. I didn't think I'd get caught.' This is the plight of those who chose to hand the reins of their lives over to the devil of immediate desires. Seduced by his promise, "You can get what you want and get away with it," they went ahead and did what they knew they shouldn't do. Yet, from the start, they were fully aware that their wants and their methods were unacceptable, because they had heard so often the wise advice and warnings from civilization's centuries of experience: its standards of right and wrong.

One supreme misconception that leads many people into trouble is the belief that they can ignore what civilization has come to regard as being wrong and get away with it unscathed. This mistaken assumption has diminished many lives and destroyed many more reputations. While it is true that some people do despicable things to fulfill their unwholesome desires and successfully avoid detection, it does not follow that one can count on that happening. Regardless, those who do escape detection do not come away from their misdeeds unharmed. At best they experience feelings of guilt coming from their own conscience. And at worst they harm themselves further whenever they quiet their troubled conscience by creating excuses and thereby relaxing their standards to the level of "anything goes." The seriousness of an evil action is not just the harm it inflicts on others. That's bad enough. But it also diminishes the person who does it. That person becomes less of a human being than is possible. And it emboldens that person to do other vile things.

First-Rate Standards

Off the coast of Labrador sometimes float huge icebergs towering three and four hundred feet into the air. Sailors have reported them moving south, directly into strong headwinds—gales blowing 30, 40, 50 knots. Yet the icebergs float onward. The explanation lies in the fact that seven-eighths of an iceberg is submerged. The great Labrador current flows strongly toward the south. It grips these frozen behemoths, carrying them steadily southward no matter how the winds might blow on the surface. And so it is with each human life. As with tall trees, lives disciplined in stabilizing standards can stand erect, unaffected by tempting winds that topple the less firmly rooted. J. C. Penney (1960), put it this way: "Second-rate standards never make a first-rate person."

Tom Phillips, who once headed Raytheon Corporation, told me of an instance where high standards saved a man in his company from almost certain ruin. During meetings at which plans were being formed to win contracts abroad, Phillips felt a strange sensation overtake him. Something deep within the depths of his heart caused him to suspect there just might be too much pressure on his people to win profitable contracts for Raytheon. "Maybe," he thought, "I ought to temper the competitive tone with a word of caution." So, he told those who were present, "We don't want any dirty money at Raytheon of any description. And, if you ever get into a situation where you have to give or get dirty money in order to win some business, the only proper thing to do is not to win that business. It is to bow out completely. And, when you come back and tell your boss that's the reason that you had to get out, that will be perfectly acceptable with Raytheon." A few years later, Phillips learned that a Raytheon sales executive who was there that day was edging very close to cutting a bad deal using payoffs. This man heeded his warnings, and because he did, he spared himself and his company trouble.

The Folly of Believing, "I Can Get Away with It"

Safety experts tell us that approximately 85 percent of all accidents are traceable to people doing dumb things—things that safety rules and common sense forbid. Another 13 percent of accidents are traceable to inadequate safety equipment, the absence of protective devices. And, only a tiny percentage of accidents are freak occurrences that no one could reasonably foresee or prevent. What's more instructive to know is that for every 1,000 dumb things people do, that is for every 1,000 unsafe acts, violating safety rules, only a tiny number ever result in accidents. Some unsafe acts result in near accidents, but in most cases nothing disastrous happens. Most of the time, people do get away with unsafe behavior.

Knowing these statistics, people in the behavioral sciences took up the question of how best to reduce industrial accidents. Their solution was to change behaviors through a process called *positive reinforcement*. This conditioning process involved rewarding people for their safe acts in small but meaningful ways. By having these people check their own behaviors and by having others sample on-the-job behaviors at work, statistics of the percentage of safe actions were recorded and made known. High scores were "rewards" in themselves and people respected these high scores. The emphasis was on safe acts, before the fact, instead of the number of days worked without the occurrence of an accident, which is a consequence of safe acts. The behavioral scientists believed that accidents would decrease if they could cause many people in literally thousands of ways to obey safety rules. And that's exactly what happened. Rewards and punishments were meted out on the basis of observed safe or unsafe behaviors, not on the frequency of accidents. The behavior-based safety management approach worked; the incidence of accidents declined noticeably. It demonstrated the effectiveness of getting employees to monitor themselves for safe behaviors and acting safely in literally thousands of seemingly small and insignificant ways.

All normal people, at one time or another, have found themselves in tempting situations with the thought running through their mind, "I can get away with doing this, although I know it is wrong. I will do it just this once." How deeply we know the folly of this approach. As with the most effective way of improving safety performance, the best way to avoid trouble is to eliminate all the many possible ways of getting oneself into trouble in the first place, even if the chances of being found out for any single occurrence of a misdeed are tiny. Someone once asked an accomplished mountain climber why he spent so much time checking and rechecking his tether lines and connecting hooks night after night, before each day's climb. "Because," he said, "When you're up there on the side of a mountain and the only thing that keeps you from falling to your death on the rocks below are those lines and hooks, you want them to be in good working order." That is how living by standards of what's right and wrong operates in our lives. Standards are the only thing holding us safe from harm. By focusing attention on creating steady habits of ethical living in thousands of small ways, a person builds a sturdy wall of reliable protection.

It is difficult to imagine anyone who would not want to avoid the many kinds of difficulties and troubles that so many others get themselves into whenever they choose to ignore ethical standards. Common sense would suggest that it's always better to be safe. Who would not want to be able to live above the fear of getting caught and the confusion of what to do when facing delicious possibilities? Everyone wants a sure defense against trouble, the security of a clean conscience, the peace of mind that comes from obeying the rules. But there is always that temptation, the belief "I can get away it, just this once." The battle we are examining here goes on in people's minds all the time. It pits one set of desires—desires for things and immediate gratification—against another set of desires—desires for a clean conscience and a good reputation. The secret of honest people lies in their strength to rise above the temptations of immediate desires. When temptations, like robbers out of the dark, leap upon them to steal their honor and peace of mind, they find protection in the safe fortress of civilization's highest standards.

When Desires Overpower Restraints

One does not have to search very far in the workplaces of the world to find examples of people whose desires overwhelmed their powers of restraint. We are all familiar with the misdeeds reported in the news media. The CEO who winks while telling underlings to do whatever is necessary to meet profit targets; the corporate officer who uses company funds for personal use and lavish parties; the chief financial officer who manipulates financial statements to hoodwink stock analysts and cause unsuspecting investors to fuel the rise of share prices; the investor with connections to corporate officers with inside information who sells stock before the share price plummets—all of these misdeeds are crowning examples of people whose desires exceeded their powers of restraint. They have neglected the elemental necessity of stabilizing standards that can hold their greedy desires and impulses in check.

A smart way of protecting oneself against attacks of any kind begins with knowledge of one's vulnerabilities. We are wise to realize that humans are most vulnerable to wrong actions where their desires are strongest. Yet what fools we are whenever we bet with our reputations and peace of mind that the guardrails of right and wrong our civilization provides for our happiness and security do not apply to us. Without restraints we allow ourselves to become slaves to our wants and victims of their recklessness.

A vivid illustration of the destructiveness of overpowering wants can be seen in what occurred several years ago. The news media reported a story about a company that had gotten itself into serious trouble because its leaders chose to disregard what smarter minds would call downright dishonesty. The miscalculated scheme began when the Beech-Nut Nutrition Corporation found itself stripped of its best money-making products.

The corporation was faced with finding a way of meeting bottom-line expectations after its parent company, Squibb, had sold off the most profitable divisions, such as chewing gum, to raise cash. After divesting themselves of other products and other divisions, the only remaining Beech-Nut division was baby food—a unit of the previous corporation that almost never earned a profit. Its arch rival was Gerber, a company that enjoyed a 70 percent market share. With only a 15 percent share of the market, Beech-Nut Nutrition, the baby food division, was incapable of matching Gerber's advertising outlays and low unit-cost structure. What's worse, Beech Nut Nutrition's market share of the dwindling baby food industry was shrinking. Finally, the parent company, Squibb, sold the Beech-Nut Nutrition baby food division to an investment group.

The new owners borrowed heavily to purchase the business. This huge debt placed added importance on immediate cash flow. So, to increase profits and boost cash returns, costs were cut. Management searched for areas to trim. One caught their eye—30 percent of the company's sales came from products containing apple concentrate. The new owners looked for a low-cost supplier and they found one: Interjuice Trading Corp., whose prices for apple concentrate were 20 percent below the market. Profit pressures were so enormous that they bought their concentrate from Interjuice.

The research and development people at Beech-Nut Nutrition were suspicious when they learned of the bargain prices. Their director wrote to top management, voicing concern. Senior officials ignored the memo. Six years later, however, the truth came out. What was supposed to have been pure apple juice concentrate was a synthetic blend—a chemical cocktail blended with real juice. Several Beech-Nut executives pleaded guilty to 215 felony counts; they had violated food and drug laws by selling adulterated apple products (*Business Week*, 1988).

Hold Yourself to the Same Standards You Expect of Others

Many workplaces are managed by people who expect behaviors of others that they are not willing to exhibit themselves. If a person is ever to achieve the distinction of standing for principles, the gravest test lies in whether he lives by those same standards himself. From his days at Ford, Robert S. McNamara was highly regarded because of his reputation for propriety. His personal actions measured as high in ethical terms as his business decisions did in thoroughness and logic. One Christmas the advertising agency that the automaker used sent gifts to many of Ford's top executives. Even though the gifts were entirely legal and the other Ford executives were pleased to accept theirs, McNamara wasn't. He returned his gift with a note—it wasn't proper for this to happen in the first place.

When he was controller at Ford, McNamara once spotted what he considered to be irregularities. He checked into them and found that some of the executives were using company airplanes and limousines for their personal travel. He had his staff track down every mile flown or driven and then he had bills sent to those corporate executives who had made use of Ford facilities without compensating the company for them. The total came to over $2 million. He told me, personally, that he billed these people for their misuse of company resources not so much to penalize them for their misbehavior but rather to establish a higher standard for expected behavior.

At another time, when McNamara was planning a skiing vacation to Aspen, he figured he'd need a car with a ski rack. A colleague suggested he use a company car in Denver. The Ford people there would be happy to put a rack on it and he could pick it up at the airport. Ford loaned out hundreds of courtesy cars to VIPs weekly. McNamara would not hear of it. Instead, he arranged to rent a car from Hertz, who would also bill him extra for the ski rack.

Fair Play

In the dog-eat-dog world of commercial competition, the high standards that most people would like to see exist are not always followed. Oftentimes, industry practices are much lower than what they ought to be. Then what should be done? The answer is to rise above common practices. You can choose to be a common person who goes by customary standards, or you can choose to operate above the ordinary, making yourself into a first-class human being.

The rule of fair play is just that. It's playing by the rules. It means not taking unfair advantage of others. And, in business this includes one's competitors! Lockheed's former chairman and CEO, Roy Anderson, once told me about a situation he faced. This situation occurred at a time when Lockheed was bidding on an overseas job. It was for a major contract worth millions of dollars. One day a competitor called him. The competitor was bothered by the fact that Lockheed had gotten hold of his company's original proposal for the contract through a business consultant. He didn't think that was fair. This was the first time Anderson heard of it, and he agreed to look into the matter.

So, Roy Anderson immediately called the division involved. "Was this true?" he asked them. "Do you have a copy of our competitor's proposal?" "Yes," they did, came the reply. They had obtained a copy of the competitor's proposal from a consultant. Then Anderson asked them one question: "Do you think that it's fair for you to be making a proposal?" Lockheed returned the competitor's original proposal and withdrew from the bidding.

The foreign government that had invited competitive bids came back to Lockheed and said, "We want you to make a proposal." So, Anderson called the competitor back and said, "They are after me to make a proposal. What do you want me to do?" The two talked for a while and agreed on a solution. Anderson went to the foreign government and told them that Lockheed would not make a proposal unless their competitor was likewise invited to submit a new proposal.

The Contagion of High Standards

Occasionally, I have wondered what it is exactly that has convinced so many people that right and wrong exist apart from what these people want or might feel like doing. Although I have no statistical data to prove it, I believe the answer is rather simple. These people observed their parents and others conforming to what they, themselves, believed to be right. When elders hold themselves accountable to standards—the same ones they expect youngsters to live by—it evokes respect for standards. And if neighbors actively guide themselves by these same basic standards, it makes their importance even more convincing. A great amount of confusion would be eliminated if we had more disciplined lives setting good examples. This is why, more than anything else, being a good parent, a good teacher, a good leader, a good boss, a good friend, involves setting a good example. I think the choicest gift we can give others is ourselves acting at our finest.

Israel Cohen, who began a grocery business in Washington, D.C., knew the importance of setting a good example, particularly with his employees. I believe, partly because of it, his Giant Food grocery stores grew to become among the largest chains in the country. Here's a small glimpse of how Cohen lived day to day.

Years ago, at lunchtime, Mr. Cohen would frequently go to the dairy section in his store, pick up several fresh eggs, and conspicuously pay for his purchase at the checkout lane, just like his customers did. A young lad who worked for Cohen would sometimes join him for lunch next door at a luncheonette, where he usually ate. The young boy was puzzled by Cohen's purchases. He asked him about this: "Mr. Cohen, why did you buy those eggs? They're yours."

Israel Cohen answered, "That's exactly why I bought them. Everyone should see that everything that goes out of this store is paid for, no matter."

Thinking with honesty and choosing the best paths to follow based on high standards—that's integrity. It is following the established rules that humankind has come to honor through centuries of experience. And it's the best way to convince others that honesty ought to be honored.

I learned about one company's experience with this great idea a few years back when I visited Charles Lazarus, perhaps the most energetic man I have ever met. He started Toys "R" Us, which at one time was the largest chain of toy stores in the world. Charles Lazarus told me about his company's "load and count" policy, something that developed out of a mistake by one of their suppliers.

In the early days when manufacturers would ship entire railroad cars of merchandise to Toys "R" Us, the railroad insisted that the receiver accept the shipper's "load and count." Whatever the shipper said was loaded and counted, that's what the buyer had to pay.

One day a large order of bicycles arrived at the receiving department warehouse. After they were unloaded and counted, someone noticed that there were three more bicycles in the rail car than the shipper billed them for. What should Toys "R" Us do about it? What would the boss, Mr. Lazarus, decide to do?

Now, it's easy to see that if you or I got shortchanged, we'd squawk about it. But if the seller made a mistake and gave us more than we are being billed for, then what should we do? There is something called temptation, and it is always asking us to make an exception for ourselves. It would be so easy to shut up about the undercount of bicycles. Not Charles Lazarus. He immediately decided to say "no" to this temptation. Lazarus ordered his purchasing department to pay the manufacturer for whatever was sent. If they sent three or four more items than they thought they sent, then the extras should be paid for. And that's exactly what they did. Did this have an effect on the company? You bet it did!

His employees loved the decision. They felt that they worked for an honest company. They learned that their boss was going to honor the same rules of honesty by which they were expected to live. There were no exceptions or excuses to be made for anyone. Because of this practice, suppliers now take the word of Toys "R" Us. Whatever they say is the actual number of units shipped, it's accepted without question.

Openness Brings Integrity

In his novel *East of Eden*, John Steinbeck captured an important truth when he wrote that observers are unwelcome visitors when people are secretly ashamed of what they're doing. In fact, said Steinbeck, the wrongdoers may even conclude that the observers are the source of their troubles in the first place. I cannot think of anything that discourages wrongdoing better than openness. The most ethical people I know use this idea in their lives everyday. It's a habitual way of thinking with them. If there is something they would not be proud to have others see them do, then they don't do it. Many in business live by what's called the *New York Times* test. We can all take this test: Ask yourself whether you would feel ashamed if what you are thinking of doing were to be printed on the front page of the *New York Times*. If you can pass that test, then it's probably okay to go ahead and do what you are thinking of doing.

"Tell them the truth," said Paul Galvin, founder of Motorola, who insisted on honesty and fair play with the company's distributors, "first because it's right and second they'll find out anyway. If they don't find it out from us we'll be the ones to suffer" (Petrakis, 1965). One thing we know about the truth is that it always comes into view at some time, either immediately or much later. Therefore, it makes good sense to expose it and the sooner and more completely done the better.

David Kearns, who once headed Xerox, told me, "Our experience has been, every time you're better off to get the truth out because it's best for the company. I also think it is right. From an overall relationship perspective you are better off. If you are up front with things you can deal with them much better."

Up-front dealings and open disclosures dissipate doubts and suspicions and false accusations better than practically anything else. I suppose it stems from the elementary idea that openness allows us to see something for ourselves and nothing is so convincing as what we have seen ourselves.

Some time ago the Caterpillar Tractor Company was accused by one of its competitors of "dumping" in the French and Spanish markets. "Dumping" in this context means selling products in foreign markets for less than what it costs a company to make them. By producing large volumes of product, average costs are lower. This is because fixed costs are spread over a larger number of units produced. This allows firms to capture a greater gross margin on products sold at home, which more than offsets the small loss incurred on those "dumped" abroad.

The French equivalent of the IRS in the United States received the charges against Caterpillar and decided to investigate them. The French government's auditors went to Caterpillar's European manager in France, where the machinery was being produced. They told Caterpillar, "We can ask for your invoices to your French dealer and your invoices for your product manufactured here to the Spanish dealer, but we can't ask for their invoices to their customers or your invoices to your selling agent in Geneva. But," they said, "if we could get the invoices all the way down the chain, then we could have the whole story. We can't legally ask for that."

Caterpillar's European manager dealt with their request openly. He told the auditors, "You can have anything you want. I will give you a serial number of any machine that's been manufactured here which we have sold to our merchandising company in Geneva, which in turn has sold it to our dealers in France or Spain. And then, if you want, I'll give you the invoice from the dealer to the customer."

The French officials asked him, "Can you get that kind of control from your dealer?" The European manager said, "They'll respond if we request it, because we review the dealer's transactions. We want to be sure that everything is going as it should be." The French officials got the information they needed and concluded that the charges were without merit. They dismissed the complaints.

Watch Out for the Interests of the Other Person

One of the surest ways of gaining an upper hand on your wants, putting them in their place so they won't overpower your good judgment, is to get into the habit of thinking first about the other person. The trouble with many people is that they seem to worry first about themselves and then, if it occurs to them at all, they consider the other person. Can you imagine how many difficulties would be avoided if the pattern were the other way around?

Jim Casey not only started and built UPS into a giant corporation, but he also made several profound observations about effective business practices. One in particular applies to overcoming greed. Casey said, "I sometimes think it unfortunate that so many kinds of business transactions must be measured in terms of money. For in each transaction involving money, our selfish motives are apt to take possession of us and tempt us to act in a way detrimental to someone else. We may easily fail to recognize that our obligations run two ways, in that we should give and get full value for every penny exchanged" (United Parcel Service, 1985).

Another illustration of this amazing principle comes from a story told to me by Walter Haas, Jr. who ran Levi Strauss & Company in San Francisco for many years, just as his father had done before him. Shortly after World War II, a man named Stafford and his son, from Sedalia, Missouri, called on the senior Haas. The Staffords had a business, the J. A. Lamy Manufacturing Company, and they were looking for contract production. Could their firm sew Levis on contract? Haas and Stafford talked for a while and struck an agreement: J. A. Lamy Manufacturing would produce a hundred dozen trousers a day. Stafford and Haas shook hands and the bargain was sealed.

That evening on their drive home after work Walter Haas, Jr. asked, "Dad, I saw the figures you agreed to with the Staffords and I know we could have gotten that production for ten cents a dozen less than you agreed to pay." The elder Haas replied, "Of course. I could have probably done better than that. What you have to understand, son, is that when you make a contract with someone, both sides have got to be happy with it. And, they are happy with it. And because they're happy with it, I expect that one of these days we'll get another five hundred dozen in that plant." A few years later, they did.

The practice of looking at business situations from the other person's side of the bargaining table is one of the best ways to succeed. It not only safeguards us against greed, it also improves relationships. This is not an idealistic theory; it's a practical guide that works. Consider the story of Cyrus H. McCormick. McCormick was fundamentally an inventor, not a businessman. Still, his concerns included customers. He wanted them, the farmers, who bought his reapers, to succeed. This approach proved to be the pivotal cause of his success.

McCormick's early attempts to license the manufacture of his reaper were disastrous. The few that were built did not perform well because of poor workmanship. It nearly ruined him. McCormick went to Chicago; there he met William Butler Ogden. With Ogden's financial backing in 1847, McCormick got a new start. With it he also insisted on how his customers were to be treated—fairly.

Every machine would be sold, without haggling, at the fixed price of $120. For $30 down and the promise to pay the balance within six months, a farmer could have one of McCormick's labor-saving machines. McCormick refrained from the common practice in those days of hiring lawyers to collect from slow-paying farmers whose crop yields were poor or who were down on their luck. Manufacturers used scare tactics and whatever fear-inducing methods they might concoct to force payment of accounts due. McCormick wouldn't.

His competitors thought he was foolish for not squeezing slow-paying farmers. "He'll get caught holding the bag," they said. The critics were dead wrong. McCormick's formula for success proved to be a strong inducement for farmers to buy his reapers. Demand grew to the point that they sold as fast as he could build them. He mowed down his competitors as his business expanded.

Living by First-Rate Standards

If we worked as hard making ourselves into first-rate persons as we do trying to achieve success, we would surely become magnificent specimens. Here are several practical ways a person can make positive strides toward that end.

1. Recognize that second-rate standards never make a first-rate person.

2. Believe that it is smarter to go by the rules; getting away with misdeeds is risky and harmful to oneself in the long run.

3. Know where your wants are strongest, because it is in these areas you are most vulnerable to letting down your standards.

4. Hold yourself to the same standards that you expect of others.

5. Approach work situations like a game and play fair, by the rules.

6. Set a good example so others have a stronger likelihood of living by high standards themselves.

7. Practice the concept of "openness," acting in ways that you would be proud to have others see.

8. Look out for the interests of others. Make sure the other person in a business deal is treated fairly.

CHAPTER 7

Stand Tall

Develop backbone and courage to do the right thing

Courage, like a high-performance engine able to pull heavy loads up steep grades and accelerate rapidly to escape harm, is indispensable to successful living. Many a life has stalled out or sits wrecked along life's highways for lack of courage. You never know when your courage will be tested. When everything depends on your performing the difficult but you'd just as soon take the easier path, you'll need courage. When your reputation and self-respect hinge on whether you bravely stand up for causes that could cost you dearly, you'll need courage in ready reserve to call upon at a moment's notice. And the strength of your courage in these difficult times will either make you or break you. Courage comes in all forms and finds expression in practically every kind of situation. And when it is observed, it is universally applauded by all well-meaning persons, particularly when life and well-being hang in the balance. Courage is the stuff of stories that have always won people's hearts. It is the source of bravery.

How differently is received the advice from persons who have actually lived though situations than is advice from those who have only imagined them. Nothing is as convincing as experience. The person who can say, "This is what I did, and this is how it turned out and why," is always more believable than the person who can only offer theories of how things should be done. One example of the power of courageous adherence to high standards worth mentioning unfolded during a panel discussion that I moderated on ethics in business several years ago. And it was demonstrated by a person of vast practical experience at the highest level.

Toward the end of the session one of the students there raised an oft-asked question: "Isn't it all right for companies operating abroad to pay bribes to get someone's business?" Some in attendance voiced the frequently heard adage, "When in Rome, do as the Romans." The implication was clear. Go ahead unthinkingly, and pay what's asked for. "What's so bad about that? You do what you have to do," they said. The role of moderator in a discussion is to facilitate discussion, not to be a discussant. I remained quiet, hoping someone would state the opposite point of view. I felt confident that someone there would surely take a stand against this shady practice but no one did—at least not immediately. Just as I was about to interject my thoughts, something unforgettable happened.

A man dressed in a dark brown business suit seated near the back of the room stood up. Everyone there knew who he was. It was John Smale, recently retired chairman and CEO of Cincinnati-based Procter & Gamble. All that morning, stories were swirling that Mr. Smale was about to be named chairman of the board of ailing General Motors. And, a few hours later, as a matter of fact, he was. But John Smale had something important he wanted to say in response to the opinions expressed embracing bribery. I think he stood up to be heard and to make an impression. He didn't want there to be any mistake about what he had to say or any confusion over how strongly he felt about it.

In a steady, convincing voice, Mr. Smale spoke: "You don't have to pay bribes to do business abroad. We [Procter & Gamble] do business all over the world and we don't pay bribes. You just don't do it!" With that, he sat down. Silence overcame those present for a moment, as each of us reflected on what had just been said. And there wasn't the slightest bit of doubt in anyone's mind there that he meant every word of it. I learned in that moment one of the key reasons why he was such an effective leader—he had backbone.

The Real Test Is in the Doing

It is a great day in any life when a person takes a stand that elicits admiration. Whenever a person stands tall in any difficult situation, word of it spreads. Others quickly learn who that courageous person is and what that person stands for. We can also be sure that something else flows from the same fountain of a person's courageous act. Their example leads others to aspire to high standards, too.

Many years ago the managing director of Caterpillar's European operations in Grenoble, France, was desperately looking for a suitable apartment. The housing there for Americans at the time was very hard to come by. The city was bulging. Decent accommodations were not to be found.

He persisted to look for an apartment to buy. One was finally located, a brand-new, seven-room suite on the sixth floor of the Park Hotel. When they finally got to negotiating the final price, which had tentatively been agreed to previously, the negotiator for the seller brought up something else. He said, "Well, of course, there's the accommodating payment to give you priority to get this apartment." It was the first time anything like that had been brought up. At that, Wally, the managing director, merely got up and said, "The meeting's adjourned. I don't want your apartment." And he walked out. That particular example permeated the whole community. Everyone knew from then on that whenever they dealt with Caterpillar, in general, or Wally, the managing director, in particular, everything would be on top of the table.

The possibilities for taking courageous stands are many, and quite frequently they might appear insignificant. But they are not insignificant, because by doing the right thing in small ways, we make possible the bigger prize we most need if we are ever to have the kinds of lives that mean something and that are worth living, our human dignity. Consider the case where an employee witnessed an unpleasant scene. A manager from one unit berated an employee publicly, yelling and cursing at this person. The event upset the observer from a different department, who, after thinking about this disturbing episode, went to the out-of-control manager and said something that needed saying. She explained how the shouting upset her and why she thought it was inexcusable and in very bad form. To his credit, the manager apologized. Perhaps hers was a minor action. Still, it was a major victory for her self-dignity.

Stand Tall for Your Standards

The gravest test of courage comes whenever a person has to take a stand and carry though with it when it is terribly inconvenient or very costly to do so. One way or another the world forces each of us into one of these kinds of situations and how we act when they occur will either make us or break us. One of the most ethical and financially savvy businessmen I ever met, Jack Reichert, who headed up the Brunswick Corporation, did many things that demonstrated a commitment to quality and meeting obligations to customers. Several years ago Brunswick came out with a new, high-performance bowling ball. These balls were an instant success. They were picked up by professionals who were winning tournaments. The country's best bowlers were endorsing these wonderful bowling balls. But, success was short lived. The balls were found to be susceptible to heat. Left in the trunk of a car on a hot day, the cover would soften. It is impossible to bowl with a marshmallow! Upon learning of the problem, Jack Reichert, responded immediately: "Recall every ball."

Corporate accountants scurried in to Reichert's office with their calculations. It could cost Brunswick over a million dollars. Reichert persisted, "Good, recall them all with a full cash refund to customers." By the time all refunds were made, the cost to Brunswick totaled $2.5 million. Reichert's words throughout the ordeal sounded loud and clear, "If our name means anything to a customer, when you make a mistake you've got to pay for it."

At Goodyear, a simple slogan has guided corporate-wide decision making there for a long time: "Protect Our Good Name." It encapsulates a basic standard that encourages all employees from top to bottom to do the right thing. When he was Goodyear's chairman and CEO, Robert Mercer boldly lived by this motto.

Once, when visiting a Goodyear tire plant in New Delhi, India, Mercer noticed that the tires being made there were substandard. They didn't have the appearance and performance of Goodyear tires that were made in other parts of the world. As a consequence, the Indian market wasn't buying Goodyear tires. Goodyear's market share had dropped from first place to sixth place in India because of it, despite being there over 60 years. Quality leadership had given way, taking a back seat to price competition and trying to do things at the least cost. Mercer believed in Goodyear's slogan. He felt that quality must come first.

Speaking to the plant's manager and staff, Mercer said, "What's happening here, fellows?"

And they said, "Well, what do you mean?"

Pointing to a tire just off the line, Mercer continued, "That tire should not have the Goodyear name on it. It should never leave this factory, because it's not up to our specifications."

The plant manager said, "Well, that's the best we can do with the equipment that we've got." There wasn't any argument about that fact. They had old machines that needed to be replaced.

Mercer said, "If it's going to carry our good name, it's got to start with our quality and performance level. Shut down every piece of equipment you've got in this plant that is incapable of producing a product that meets our specifications."

The plant manager kind of stared at him for a moment. He wanted to call somebody in Akron, Ohio, but it dawned on him that there wasn't anybody higher up in the organization than the man who had just issued the directive. The plant manager said, "Do you realize I've already shut down 40 percent of the plant?"

Mercer was unmoved by the plant manager's excuse; it seemed lame to him. He said, "Let me tell you something, my friend. I'm trying to figure out whether we ought to shut down the entire plant and get rid of it and just pull out of India as a manufacturing facility. I'm just leaning this way to let this operation continue, so let's not challenge this. I want it done."

The plant manager shut down the entire plant. Mercer knew that they could get the job done if they had the right equipment, and $4 million was spent replacing faulty and worn out machines. Today that plant is turning out good-quality products, and the spirit, attitude, and pride of the people there are all high.

Not "Can I?" but "Ought I?"

A page from the life story of J. C. Penney reveals the source of a business principle that served him well. It had to do with a lesson he learned while trying to sell watermelons. At 17, an age when most boys enter their senior year of high school, young J. C. Penney had already developed an entrepreneurial flair. His summer's crop was bountiful and prices were good. An average melon went for a nickel and the largest ones brought a dime. Young Jim Penney felt he was going to make out well, selling the melons he had raised. He rented a horse and wagon and began driving throughout his town, peddling his crop.

Then one Saturday he got an idea. The county fair was opening that day. There would be lots of people eager to enjoy a slice of refreshing watermelon for sure. So, he drove his wagon as near to the main entrance as he could get it and began selling melons. His plan was short lived, however. Feeling a hand on his shoulder young Penney heard his father's voice: "Better go home, son. Go on—now!"

Bewildered and embarrassed, Jim Penney obeyed. His father followed a few minutes later. Arriving home, the senior Penney found Jim in front of their house sitting on the wagon, his head slumped down.

"Do you know why I told you to go home?" his father asked him.

"No, sir." Jim didn't know.

"Did it mean anything to you that the fair was supported by concessions?"

Again, Jim answered, "No."

His father explained that everyone inside the fair grounds had paid a concession fee.

"But I wasn't selling inside the grounds," young Jim argued.

"That's just it," his father said. "Without paying anything toward the support of the fair, you were taking advantage of those who did. Everyone is entitled to earn a living, you and everyone else, but never by taking advantage of others" (Beasley, 1948).

There is a simple guide that anyone might want to consider when facing a tough choice, especially if there might be a questionable ethical aspect to it. It is this: Humans are creatures who can ask of each of their actions not just, "Can I do it?" but "Ought I do it?" No amount of affirmative answers to the first question can balance a negative answer to the second.

In trying to become a strong-willed person with the courage to stand tall for what's right and good, it is useful to be aware of a misleading idea. We hear so often that good ethics is really just good business. Now, this is largely true. It is good for a business to do the ethical thing because it keeps so many troubles away. It pays in the marketplace in the long run, because the practice builds confidence and attracts customers. But consider the implications of this charming saying—good ethics is good business—and you'll discover it rests on a pathetic argument, utterly lacking in character. When you think about it, the person who justifies ethical behavior simply because it pays is always looking out for self, first and foremost. How do you suppose that person will choose when an unethical scheme comes along? Will it be to do what's right because it's right, or will it be to do what pays?

The world is hungry for solid men and women who gladly set high standards ahead of immediate gain. These people operate on a higher plane and they sleep well at night because of it. Here is a useful test that anyone can use as a guide when facing one of these kinds of choices. Ask yourself, "Am I choosing what I'd be proud of doing or am I choosing something because it will pay off?" It all comes down to what is in your heart, causing you to be mindful of the payoff or the principle as you choose.

Courage Earns Confidence

A good reputation not only wins the confidence of others; it also attracts the right sorts of people and business opportunities. Temptations, which would otherwise present themselves to a person, tend to stay away, so strong is the good reputation of the person of high standards. What's more, opportunities generally flow toward the centers of confidence. People prefer to do business with straight shooters. A firm that has the courage to set high ideals and live up to them attracts good people. If those people have the backbone to live by these standards, then customers will be attracted to do business with that firm.

A good reputation does something else. It speaks out in subtle ways, saying, "If you aren't decent and honorable, we won't have anything to do with you." Here's an illustration. The James River Corporation was founded by two men, Brenton S. Halsey and Robert C. Williams, who, from the start, saw the need to establish certain values and beliefs to guide the growth and direction of their expanding firm. They sought an honorable identity for the growing company that they were building. The co-founders realized that they had a unique opportunity to establish a new identity for their new company, to establish values and beliefs as they wanted. One of the first things they did was to write down what they believed, the values and beliefs by which they wanted their company to operate. The first and most important one they identified was ethics. The co-founders were competitive. There was no mistaking that. They played hard to win the business game. But like any other game, they believed you "win" by playing by the rules.

It wasn't long before their commitment to ethical business dealings got tested. Filter papers for the automobile industry represented one of the highest gross margin product lines that James River Paper produced. It was the cornerstone of their move to profitability. James River, as is true with many firms starting out, had losses during its early days. So, they needed to sell more of the higher-profit margin lines of papers. One day a buyer with whom they were dealing approached them. He demanded something extra, under the table, if his company was going to purchase from James River. The co-founders were dumbfounded by the buyer's blatant demand. And they didn't like it one bit. They told him in no uncertain terms, "No, thank you. If that's required, we'll find some other way to sell our products." While it was difficult for them to turn down good business, it was not difficult for them to stand tall for their principles. Now the interesting thing is what happened to James River Paper as a result of this.

By having the courage to operate business on a highly ethical plane, they had to work extra hard to earn a reputation for extraordinary product quality and top-notch customer service. These efforts led to a competitive advantage. Their products and service were so good that asking for kickbacks was out of the question. Competing on "real" value proved to be the best way for their growing company to gain sales and increase its market share. Had they tried getting sales through kickbacks, it's doubtful whether they'd still be a profitable business in such a competitive industry.

Get Out in Front of Ethical Lapses and Fix Them

The consequences of ignoring ethical failures are usually disastrous. The smartest thing to do whenever an ethical lapse is revealed is to set matters straight with those who have been harmed or could be harmed and show that the failures will not happen again. In 1987, a scathing story broke about Chrysler. It was something that could have erupted into a major scandal for the giant automaker, struggling to survive. Word got out that up until October 1986, managers at assembly plants drove new cars home and back supposedly to sample production quality. These cars were later sent to dealers and sold as new, with no hint that employees had driven them for up to 400 miles. This was not all. Some of the cars had been damaged during the tests. Regardless, Chrysler repaired and sent them to dealer showrooms where they were sold as new anyway.

At a press conference following the news, cynical reporters were on hand with sharply worded questions for Chrysler's chairman and CEO, Lee Iacocca. He wasn't there to hoodwink customers or skirt the issue. Iacocca faced it head-on with candor and contriteness: "Did we screw up?" he asked, rhetorically. "You bet we did," he said. He admitted the practice was true. Chrysler employees had disconnected odometers on over 60,000 test cars. This, Iacocca said, "went beyond dumb and reached way out to stupid." The chairman didn't stop there. The next morning two-page ads appeared in major newspapers admitting the mistake: "Testing cars," the ad read, "is a good idea. Disconnecting odometers is a lousy idea. That's a mistake we won't make again at Chrysler. Period."

To make things right with buyers who had purchased the vehicles "tested," Chrysler extended its 5-year or 50,000-mile warranties on engine and power-train to 7 years or 70,000 miles. These extended warranties included brakes, suspension, air conditioning, electrical, and steering, just to put their buyers' minds at ease. Chrysler offered free inspections, and they offered to replace any vehicle that was damaged in testing with a brand new 1987 Chrysler Corpo-ration model of comparable value. No ifs, ands, or buts.

Attempts to conceal problem areas and wrongdoing are incapable of negat-ing their existence. History is lavish in examples of people who miscalculated that they could cover their tracks. Regardless of how hard a person tries to hide something, sooner or later the truth always comes out anyway.

Stand Up for Others Who Cannot Stand Up for Themselves

Several years ago, James Eiszner, who was president, chairman, and CEO of CPC International at the time, a major foods company, wondered aloud with me about a knotty personnel problem that had plagued his organization earlier. What made this problem particularly difficult was the fact that it pitted some of the brightest up-and-comers in his company against a group of old-timers. Whenever employees are abroad in foreign assignments for many years, they can grow obsolete, especially if they are away twenty, thirty, or more years in less-developed parts of the world. When they're brought back to the states, they have difficulty fitting in. It's hard, as U.S. companies have found, to find places back home for these people. CPC International faced this problem.

With a downturn in its foreign businesses, it became necessary to sell off some of their international operations and bring American CPC International em-ployees back to the states. Many of these folks were assigned to one section of the company that was expanding rapidly. It was the best spot in which CPC had to place these older employees. The younger employees there, the high per-formers—they were business school trained MBAs—couldn't understand why CPC was "carrying" these people. They called the unit to which many of them were assigned the "elephant graveyard." The high performers went to their bosses and complained: "You pay me well and I do my job well; but you are paying these laggards well, too, and they don't perform. This just isn't right." They just couldn't understand why the company was carrying them.

Dr. Eiszner explained to these younger employees that there is more to man-aging a business than just cold dollar-and-cents profit concerns. There are human concerns, too. He told the complainers, "These people have given us twenty or thirty years of very dedicated service, doing the best they could. Now their contributions are diminishing. Regardless, we have to give them an opportunity to blend back in at home. We ought to be fair to them for all the service they've given this company. We owe them for that."

Put Principles Ahead of Immediate Gains

Ample evidence exists that doing the right thing is good for business. Acts of good citizenship help win community support, which comes in handy when a firm needs the cooperation of local leaders. A company that markets top-quality products and stands behind those that fail to perform as promised is a company that holds on to customers and attracts others. The fair treatment of suppliers brings a business loyal service and ensures timely deliveries. Humane treatment of employees yields dedication, loyalty, and satisfaction—things that translate into better profits. But none of these reasons are based on courage. They are merely pragmatic justifications, a quid pro quo arrangement. Whenever pragmatism is given as the justification for acting morally, it is abundantly clear what remains uppermost in the person's heart. That isn't courage; it is crude materialism dressed up in alluring disguise.

The powerful business principle (mentioned in Chapter 6) that Cyrus McCormick applied was this: no one is foolish when he stops to consider others. Actually, most people's troubles spring from the opposite approach. I've never seen a situation or a business relationship that has been harmed by this simple act of consideration. In most every case it proves beneficial. Take the story about a salesman for Deluxe Check Printers.

Many years ago and before checks were personalized with the customer's name printed on them, people used bank checks. In those days, banks bought these checks in large quantities. They'd buy maybe a half a year's supply at one time, with the bank's name printed on them. A newly hired salesman for Deluxe Check Printers in St. Paul, Minnesota, eager to do well, took an order from a West Coast bank—5 million checks! He was so elated with his huge order that he called his company's president, George McSweeny, to tell of his windfall.

Stunned by the news, McSweeny asked the salesman, "Five million checks? What is the size of the bank?" The salesman told him, and McSweeny responded, "Well, that will be more checks than they'll need for several years. You go back and tell him he should cut that order back to less than a million. And give him the reasons why—they could spoil or be damaged. The bank's routing number could be changed." The salesman did just as he was told. The bank president was flabbergasted. Now the next time this bank needed checks, from whom do you suppose they bought?

Have the Backbone to Live above the Ordinary

Anyone who has lived in the thick of life knows the pull of easier and more expedient paths. At one time or another, each of us confronts a situation where we can ignore the problem and let things slide or react in ways that actually add to the difficulty. How we react in the face of these difficulties reveals our backbone and character. Here are two examples.

Many years back, some salespeople from Levi Strauss & Company came to their superiors with a problem. A competitor's sales force was telling retailers untrue stories about Levi products. They were telling them that the quality of Levi products was dropping and that the Levi organization was not supporting its product and promises of delivery. Bear in mind that the apparel industry is hotly competitive. A percentage shift in sales up or down makes a huge difference in bottom-line results. The Levi organization had a long-held tradition of not "trashing" its competition. In fact they had then (and they still do now) a policy of not saying anything bad about their competitors or their competitors' products. Nevertheless, in the face of this competitor's tactic, Levi sales were being harmed. What were Levi's salespeople to do? Should they stand by and let it happen, or retaliate in a like manner?

Now, we all have had this same sort of thing happen to us. Someone says terrible things about us, causing us to get mad. And in the heat of anger, our natural reaction is to want to fight back. "Okay," we might feel like saying, "If that's the way you want to play, let's see how you like this . . . ." And so, we go on the attack. But civility involves taking control of one's life; it frequently demands our saying "no" to flashes of rage and impulsive actions that are sure to turn destructive later. Such a decisive element in character is this matter of self-control, built-in strength from many years of disciplined habits. To have it in good working order and at one's disposal on short notice is generally a distinguishing factor in a person's life. This is what helped the people at Levi Strauss & Company do the right thing. They lived by a simple principle that whenever one feels rage, it is always safe advice to remember that it never pays to kick a skunk.

Highly successful business people know that it is far better to compete in a realm that really matters—on product quality and customer service—than on cheap tricks that can easily be duplicated by even the common street thug. Levi managers stuck to the high road. Their response was, "Don't say anything negative about the competition. Let Levi quality and dependability reveal itself. Point out our product's quality to the retailers. Demonstrate to them through what we do that we are reliable. Let our product quality and our actions speak for themselves."

Encourage Others to Stand Tall

We do well to recognize the fact that it is really the accumulation of many little things that build us into who we are. It is the unthinking, habit-formed decisions we make daily that form ourselves and, through that process, form our strength of character to respond admirably when really big temptations come our way.

We can be challenged to stand tall for lofty ideals at unexpected times and in unexpected ways. We can also be called upon to help others do the same thing. I'd like to illustrate this idea with another story about Robert McNamara that he told me; it happened to him when he attended a state dinner. At a round table where he sat, there was a woman on either side of him and a man on the left of the woman on his left. During the meal, this man leaned across her and said, "Bob, I'd like your help. I've got to decide this afternoon whether to pay $2 million to the Shah's sister. They've sent us two billion-dollar orders. Bob, what should I do?" In the first place, McNamara didn't recognize the man. Second, he certainly was not going to speak in front of the woman, whom he didn't know either. So, he said, "I'm terribly sorry, it's outside my experience." Afterwards, the man approached McNamara and repeated what he had said. By then, McNamara recognized him. He was the president of a company that was in competition for orders that might well have been worth $2 billion. McNamara looked him in the eye and said, "At Ford I came across this situation. We never paid a dime to my knowledge. I'd tell him [the Shah] to go to hell. And frankly, I hope that's what you'll do."

When we think about it, we realize that true leaders don't gain stature from clever schemes. They earn leadership status from authentic commitments to what's decent and fair—to what people feel most proud to honor. And, thoughtful people naturally respect doing the "right thing." But one caution—this is not something these leaders do because it returns benefits. They do what's right because they believe it should be done, because they genuinely feel higher concerns call for it. And they have the backbone to insist on it. This is what leadership is all about—isn't it? It is the process of influencing others.

Having the Backbone to Stand Tall

Here are several useful suggestions for applying the main ideas in this chapter.

1. Courageously stand up for what's right, despite what it might cost you.
2. Be more concerned about what you ought to do than you are with what you can do.

3. Realize that courageous stands bring about confidence, confidence in yourself and confidence of others in you.

4. Fix ethical lapses and errors immediately.

5. Protect others who cannot protect themselves.

6. Put principles ahead of immediate gains.

7. Act in ways that lead others to have courage and backbone.

CHAPTER 8

Act Boldly on Your Convictions

Don't be frozen by fears

When facing decisions or considering opportunities that beg for immediate action, many people find themselves frozen, unwilling to move on. One reason is the "fearful child" who lurks deep within their personality. These people are in constant dread of receiving a scolding from any critical outsider. Their dominating motive is not achievement but the avoidance of ridicule. They will do anything to escape hearing "I told you so" from others. To prevent the slightest possibility of criticism, these people continually insist on gathering more information and doing further study before moving ahead. They consider every conceivable possibility but never commit themselves to a course of action. They stall out. When others notice their indecisiveness and inaction, these people have a ready excuse—"We need to be sure before we decide or act; the cost of making a mistake is simply too great." They defend their timidity by complimenting themselves, insisting that their approach is really an insignia of intelligence and open mindedness. "After all," they think to themselves, "I must be far smarter than you because I am willing to consider more possibilities and spend more time analyzing all the nuances involved. I'm truly a deeper thinker." In reality these people care more about not being wrong than they do about achieving concrete results.

To be sure, the "fearful child" who's alive in all normal, well-adjusted persons can serve a useful purpose. All wise people understand the folly of ill-considered moves. They know that good decisions require consideration of all the possibilities and their implications. And they try not to invite failure to come their way by proceeding without adequate forethought. The secret of the successful accomplisher, however, lies in knowing when to strike a balance between deciding and not deciding, between taking an action and not taking any action at all. When the "fearful child" dominates a person, it intimidates, paralyzing the powers of choice and action. It causes people to become overly concerned with failure and criticism. And by raising one's worry of making mistakes out of proportion, it prevents any possibility of progress.

Honesty enables people to accept the truth—living is neither easy nor certain. While a person may be open minded and try to obtain all the relevant information about a situation before moving forward, honesty forces that person to recognize the risks of waiting too long or not acting at all. Ours is a world of vast unknowns and things unknowable. There are no sure things. The truth is that some actions must be taken on the basis of what one believes. There is no way of knowing with certainty whether a marriage, or an investment, or a new project, or an untried approach, or a new product or method, or countless other possibilities will work out. Boldness is the quality that wise people everywhere recognize as an indispensable force within their personality that holds the "fearful child" in check, enabling them to move ahead. Boldness is the willingness to bet one's wealth and reputation that a believed-in course of action will work. And it is from this belief that a human being derives the imagination and fortitude to do whatever is needed along the way to make their venture succeed in the grip of difficulties.

Unhesitating Commitment

One of the most useful skills people can develop as they move through life is to be able start a venture and then, unhesitatingly, give their best efforts to make it work. Suppose your company had just spent 39 months and $1.6 billion creating a new family of cars—a bold move that in all likelihood will determine whether your firm remains a major player in the hotly competitive auto industry. But now an unforeseen problem arises shortly after you ship the first 4,000 of these vehicles: a washer on the suspension system of one car breaks during a test drive training session. Quality reputation is all important for these new-from-the-ground-up designed cars. What would you do?

This was the question Chrysler's chairman, Lee Iacocca, had to decide. Should Chrysler fix the one car, hoping the broken washer was just an isolated instance? Should they check the remaining 3,950 cars not in buyers' hands and quietly recall the 50 already sold? Or, should they recall all 4,000 cars and loudly proclaim to the public what was going on? A recall risked destroying consumer confidence in the new cab-forward cars. Iacocca chose the third option. And he did it without studying reams of financial data, or hours of meetings, or excessive worry about what others might say. Why? He chose to recall all vehicles because he was boldly committed to building a reputation for product quality.

An Essential Element for Progress

Aristotle gave philosophy many ideas, one of which was that moderation is a virtue. The good life according to him is one that strikes a balance between two extremes—everything should be done in moderation. As great as Aristotle was, on this particular point history shows that he was wrong. It may be a virtue to act in moderation in some areas of life, but it does not follow that it is a virtue to act that way in all areas. In many areas moderation is a hindrance to progress.

The world of biography is rich with examples of great persons who were not guided by moderation at all but by their strong beliefs. Many of these people broke with convention and challenged the status quo. Mother Teresa did not moderate her efforts as she ministered to the poor in the slums of Calcutta. Michelangelo's efforts in sculpting and painting were not held back by moderation. General George Patton was not guided by moderation as he defeated German armies in World War II. Einstein did not pursue unlocking the mysteries of science with moderation. It is these people, not those who were moderate, who gave the world advancements. They followed their dreams, giving their finest efforts, not in moderation but wholeheartedly and without reservation.

When we examine great lives, the importance of boldness becomes strikingly clear. Georgia O'Keeffe, for example, did what few women were able to do in the early part of the twentieth century. She established a reputation as a world-acclaimed artist in what had traditionally been a man's world. Georgia O'Keeffe was strong-willed, hardworking, and whimsical. She boldly painted as she wanted to paint. Americans and the rest of the world loved her paintings. Her greatness came because she was not afraid to paint what her imagination held: the skull of a horse with a bright pink Mexican artificial flower in the eye socket; animal skulls, horns, pelvises, and leg bones that gleamed white against brilliant skies; New York skyscrapers; Canadian barns; and crosses and oversized flowers. She was not a person to be intimidated by a "fearful child" within. She painted as she pleased, and O'Keeffe sold her works for handsome prices. The avant garde, inner circle of modern American artists recognized her as being a step ahead of everyone. Her boldness enabled her to paint as she wanted to paint, even though it was out of step with the popular taste and accepted style of her time.

Any serious study of human achievement will reveal the fact that progress does not always move in a smooth, straight line. Most progress is marked by extremes. Otherwise, there is no progress. A movement or idea gets started, first pushing things in one direction, maybe a bit extreme or overdone but forward.

Then and after some time, another movement or idea catches hold, partly supported to repair the extreme parts of what's gone before but not without its own extremes. In a zigzag fashion, change comes but movement is overwhelmingly ahead, forward. Boldness gives people the ability to move forward in a direction of their choosing. It is the willingness to risk that an idea will work before one knows with certainty that it will work. It is a virtue because this willingness motivates humans to discover new knowledge and advance civilization. It also excites their finest efforts, inspiring them to give the hard work and effort required for success.

The Leap of Faith

Imagine an entrepreneur on the eve of launching a new enterprise. The products are well made. Marketers believe customers will willingly pay top dollar. Financing is in order; a sizeable line of credit from a local bank has been set up. Early marketing surveys predict positive results. The investors and the creditors have gone over the business plan many times. Will it be successful? Nobody can predict for certain. Like anything else that's never been done before, this, too, is a gamble. And now our entrepreneur starts out, buoyed with high expectations. The entrepreneur moves forward, propelled by a great leap of faith that the venture will succeed. Were this business owner to know, beforehand, all the problems, frustrations, setbacks, and difficulties that will arise, the new enterprise might never begin. Worrisome difficulties are not the focus of the bold person's attention. Turning the dream of success into a reality—that's the entrepreneur's focus.

Once any venture is begins, it will struggle. Problems will arise. Financial ruin is always possible, as obligations fall due month after month. But, once begun, there can be no turning back. Faith that the venture will succeed and a willingness to do whatever it takes become the entrepreneur's best allies. Without faith, life is limp and ill directed. If a challenge is known and moderate, experience and skill are enough; if it is unknown and nearly impossible, then only faith can muster the resolve and the wherewithal to accomplish it. We need to understand this: there are people aplenty who can do the ordinary, the possible. They can be hired for an ordinary wage. But the real rewards are for those who perform the extraordinary, the impossible.

Boldness is not gambling on poorly conceived schemes. Boldness is the abiding commitment to face whatever may come, no matter how terrible or tragic the problems are that arise. One never fully knows beforehand whether a decision or contemplated action will prove successful. Certainty eludes us all. The only way to know for sure is to try, to test, to boldly move on and implement the decision or plan.

Everyone knows Mickey Mouse, Donald Duck, and Snow White and the Seven Dwarfs. And everyone knows the name Walt Disney, their creator, who built a whimsical cartoon studio into one of the largest and most-respected entertainment empires. Any Hollywood producer would be thrilled to receive one Academy Award. Walt Disney accumulated 29 Oscars. He was not afraid of risk. His early work was a seven-minute cartoon, but that was only a start. Disney was the first to mix animation with live action. He pioneered in making feature-length cartoons that are classics, loved by today's children every bit as much as they were loved when first released decades earlier. And his nature films were nearly as popular.

Walt Disney achieved greatly because he believed greatly. He boldly dared that his ideas would appeal to audiences. And because of this level of unhesitating boldness, Walt Disney rose to defeat the skepticism he received every time his imagination foresaw new possibilities. To get his idea, Mickey Mouse, off the ground Disney had to pawn or sell everything because exhibitors looked upon the cartoon character with a high-pitched voice and red pants as just another cartoon. When he decided to make *Snow White and the Seven Dwarfs*, most Hollywood experts scoffed—"No audience would sit through a lengthy animated fairy tale," they said. It became one of the biggest money-makers in history. And, when he became the first important movie producer to make films for television, his detractors said he was a fool. And again, he proved them wrong.

In business, commitment is needed in many areas: from introducing new products to devising creative methods of advertising, from winning commitments to environmental issues to developing better accounting systems, and from introducing smarter safety methods to changing corporate cultures for the world ahead. Intelligence and ability are useful to making improvements of any significance. But it is boldness that overcomes inertia, that accepts difficulties head on, and that keeps things moving in the direction wanted.

Rise above Indifference

Among the most common of human downfalls is indifference. When infected with indifference, a person lives for what's easy and, because of that, the person adds practically nothing to human progress. Indifference comes from the desire to play it safe. But safe can never be admired. Our highest praise is reserved for those who stand tall by boldly standing up for what they believe is important.

Avon decided to sell Tiffany & Co. in 1984. One of the bidders was Donald Trump. The other was an LBO of the management. Trump came in with the highest bid and insisted that they move forward. Avon's CEO at the time, Hicks Waldron, clearly would have preferred the LBO of the management team, but as

CEO of a publicly held company he had to be concerned with how much was offered. He could lean a little in one direction but not too much. So Waldron called Trump to his office. The two men talked for about an hour and a half. Before too long, Waldron, a man not to be intimidated by an inner "fearful child," found himself lecturing Donald on the difference between Tiffany's and a skyscraper, for which Trump is famous. He told Trump, "One of the concerns I have, Donald, is that you will treat this business as a piece of property. It's not a piece of property. All you've done is sit here and talk about that building over there." Trump was going to cut a hole so you could get into Tiffany's from the first floor of Trump Tower. "If that's what you want to do, fine," said Waldron. "But what you haven't said anything about yet and what I want to talk to you about this afternoon is the entity, the organization called Tiffany. And it's alive with terrific people, whose hearts beat and throb and who have a plan in place, whose livelihoods depend upon how well that institution does, which means, therefore, how well you do owning that institution." Donald sat there and listened to the whole thing. Maybe he heard it as well. As it turned out he wasn't serious about buying, so the LBO worked out.

The main point to remember about boldness is that it involves doing what one believes ought to be done, not what's convenient or simply yields the greatest benefits. Many people have demonstrated this kind of boldness in various ways. The leaders of Levi Strauss & Company, who have long exhibited a genuine commitment to human dignity and fairness, provide a good example. Top management there has worked very hard throughout its history to make every work environment one that ennobles employees. Once Levi Strauss & Company bought out a plant in Blackstone, Virginia; all of the employees there were white. After a time the plant's manager, Paul Glasgow, came to Walter Haas, Jr., who ran Levis at the time, and said, "I think the time is right to integrate the plant."

Walter's response was, "Good. We're with you."

He then went to the leaders in that small Southern town, to make his intentions known. Glasgow learned that they wanted to divide the plant into "black" and "white" sections. Levi's management said, "No, we're not going to do that."

The town's leaders then asked for a dividing line to be painted so as to keep blacks on one side and whites on the other. And, again the company refused.

Next, separate drinking fountains and toilet facilities were requested. And again Levi said "no" to that proposal. The people at Blackstone didn't like Levi's stand; it violated their long-standing customs. An attempt was next made to pressure Levi to stop insisting on integrating its production facility. The local employment service stopped sending applicants to the plant for available jobs.

Paul Glasgow asked headquarters in San Francisco, "What will we do?" And, Walter Haas, Jr., who was chairman and CEO at the time, said, "Close the plant."

The plant didn't close. Seeing that Levi was that serious about their commitment to equal opportunity, the town's leaders backed down. It was a great victory for fairness. Because of this bold stand, the employment practices in the whole community were altered.

The Tragedy of the Unseized Moment

Many people tend to forget that life comes at us fast. Challenges and opportunities pop up and then they pass by; how we act when these times arise will go a long way in determining our reputations, our accomplishments, and our self-respect. The need for boldness seems clear: We make our marks on life by how we act in it, whether we make our moves when the times call for action. Alongside courage, boldness is a major source of action. It is the spark that ignites movements, large and small. Boldness is behind one's words of encouragement or reprimands when they are needed; boldness is behind one's willingness to recheck a report for errors or fix a production problem without waiting to be told to do so and before it fully develops into disaster.

Holding back from fully doing what we believe ought to be done—even partially—when times call for action can spell the difference between success and regret later on. I think at one time or another even the best of us are guilty of letting things slide. Roy Anderson, when he was the board chairman of Lockheed, once told me about a time, earlier, when he had failed to act and then he regretted it afterward. It wasn't that he had done something bad. It was that he had not gotten involved early enough and forcefully enough to prevent something that should have been stopped in its tracks.

He told me that he had earlier heard faint rumblings about illegal payments being made by people in his company to win business in Japan. But since these were only vague rumors, he didn't do anything about them. At the time, he later said, he felt too busy to look into these rumors. This was a costly oversight. The illegal payments were eventually discovered and a major scandal followed. In retrospect, he was sorry, realizing that he had let down himself and his company. It was one of those mistakes people sometimes make where it isn't what they do but what they don't do that matters.

Live by Your Beliefs

A tendency into which anyone can easily slip is to sit back and not take a stand because to do so would be unpopular. The "fearful child" inside tells us to avoid controversy or ridicule, whatever the cost. This is not a behavior pattern of those whom we most admire. Our highest regard is reserved for those who pursue worthy purposes and stand up for their beliefs without hesitation. These people boldly commit themselves to a clear position regardless of whether it is popular, pleasing to others, or expedient.

Dow Chemical once had a product, an agricultural chemical called 245T. It was a relatively unimportant product in terms of sales. Folks from the Environmental Protection Agency (EPA) one day banned this product on what Dow considered to be trumped-up charges. Now Dow had a simple way out—forget it. It was a minor product; they really had something better in the laboratory and they knew 245T was going to be obsolete in a few years. The proper economic decision was to say, "Good-bye, we'll not do anything about it." But Dow had 20 years of science behind this product. They knew it to be good and safe. If they let EPA ban this one on insubstantial claims, what might EPA do next? So, Dow decided to fight it. The fight went on for several years. It cost them not just money but goodwill with regulatory agencies. As they fought it, they kept saying, "Economically, this makes no sense." But Dow was standing on an important principle—scientific evidence should be respected. The main point to learn from this is that Dow chose to stand up for a deeply held principle; and they felt that doing so was more important than what would have been expedient. That's boldness at its finest.

In the 1950s, in this country, Ford was the first to introduce certain safety features in its automobiles—the collapsible steering wheel, door locks, padded visor and instrument panel, and seat belts. Ford employees looked for information on how to reduce fatalities. Their search led them to the Cornell Aeronautical Laboratories, which had been hired by the U.S. Army Air Corps in World War II. The aeronautical research unit found that more lives were being lost from automobiles than from airplanes. After the war, this research effort continued with the state police in North Carolina. Based upon their findings from accident studies, Ford introduced several safety features. However, that decision was strongly opposed by others in the industry and by some within the Ford organization. These groups argued that (1) safety doesn't sell automobiles and (2) it is a societal problem and therefore should be dealt with by society or government. Top management differed with this approach and moved boldly to do what they believed should be done; build safety features into new automobiles.

Don't Be Defeated by Your Tentativeness

Tentativeness can be useful up to a point. We can be tentative in our thoughts about what to do as we study a situation. We can be tentative about accepting hypotheses to explain phenomena in scientific studies until more data are collected. But once we make up our minds as to what to do, once we begin a venture, tentativeness can be ruinous. It is worth realizing that any undertaking of significance can be crippled by tentativeness. This is because tentativeness holds back one's full energies of commitment. Anything less than total confidence that the scheme will work tends to destroy its chances from the very start. Boldness defeats the skepticism and doubt, and the ensuing worry to which they lead, siphoning off the energy needed to carry any venture to a successful completion. Anyone can unthinkingly squander his energies on hesitation and worry when he could, otherwise, be directing his strongest efforts to make a hoped-for improvement or budding enterprise work. I once saw an example of the crippling effects of tentativeness in a baseball game, and I believe that it illustrates the nature of what happens in other endeavors, be they scientific, business, or personal.

By all accounts, the 1991 World Series had run dead even. And so, when the Minnesota Twins and the Atlanta Braves began the seventh and deciding game, the prevailing mood among fans was that it was too bad that one of these teams would have to lose the series.

As it unfolded, the series finale produced many exciting moments but no score through seven full innings. It was the longest that any seventh World Series game had ever progressed without either team scoring.

In the top of the eighth inning, the Braves at bat, Lonnie Smith led off. He singled into right field. Terry Pendleton, who would later be named his league's most valuable player, batted next. The powerful left-handed hitter, clinging to a 2 and 1 count, drove a long ball double deep into left center field.

Smith raced for second. As he neared the bag, Twins second baseman, Chuck Knoblauch, tried a decoy play, faking that he had fielded a grounder. He pretended to throw the (nonexistent) ball to shortstop Greg Gagne covering second.

This confused Smith as he rounded second base and started for third. Suddenly he held up—a dead stop. The deception had worked its trick, while the ball in play landed on the warning track and bounced high off the outfield wall. Smith's hesitation wasted precious time as the Twins' outfielder scrambled to field the ball.

Then, seeing where the ball really was, Lonnie resumed running, reaching third easily. But there was not enough time to score. The base running gaffe cost Atlanta a run and ultimately the 1991 World Series itself.

The Fruits of Boldness

Playwright Garson Kanin once asked Arthur Rubinstein, "Am I right in thinking that you're playing better now than ever before?"

"I think so," the great pianist answered.

"Is it experience, practice, what?"

"No, no, no," said Rubinstein. "I am 80. So, now I take chances I never took before. You see, the stakes are not so high. I can afford it. I used to be so much more careful—no wrong notes, not too bold ideas, watch tempi. Now I let go and enjoy myself, and to hell with everything except the music!"

I think this story has a message behind it: we are at our best when we act on our convictions without reservation—when we are not tentative or overly concerned with what others think. Our best efforts come when we do what we believe should be done—that's boldness. It is the thoughtful commitment to a position and then the gallant, steadfast will to see it through in the face of difficulty. It is the bridge from our visions to great victories. It is the great enabler.

How to Be Bold

How can you become a bold individual? First, you decide by an act of will that you will stand up for your high standards. You decide to make your actions measure up to your words. Next, you commit yourself to what you believe, not because it gives you an immediate payoff but because you believe it ought to be done, because you believe it is, on balance and in the long run, in the best interests of everyone concerned including your organization. Third, you act without hesitation, without worry over what others might say or think about you—you defeat your "fearful child" within. You act out of conviction not with the aim of expecting immediate praise or rewards. And finally, you are bold in all realms, especially where what you might do to mend a wrong or advance a good cause needs your strong backbone. Effective leaders do this all the time.

All great ventures hold great uncertainties and, as a consequence, demand great faith and the willingness to wager that the undertaking will work. It is not enough merely to believe in what one does. It is necessary to go forward and prove it by staking oneself on it and by making the dream a reality. Efforts made in management development and training, safety newsletters, "no questions asked" exchange policies, detailed quality inspection procedures, extra time given to corporate communication and employee dialogue with the firm's leaders, and equal opportunity policies are just a few of the many things done by business people, and done well and enthusiastically, because people believe they are important. Proof does not exist that these efforts will produce bottom-line benefits. Yet, they are done well and enthusiastically on the strength of the belief that they should be done.

CHAPTER 9

Be Your Own Person

Do things because they are praiseworthy,
not because they are popular

The ability that gives humans their capacity to be aware of themselves and inspect their own behavior is the same ability that allows them to visualize how others will regard them. This ability can cut two ways. As social creatures with needs for acceptance and belonging, humans generally want to be liked and appreciated. They want to fit in, to be accepted, and to enjoy whatever praise comes their way. These desires have benefits. Social forces tend to discourage antisocial behaviors and promote civility. A large measure of how people regard themselves is determined by how they think others regard them. It is very seldom, therefore, that our finest actions arise from absolutely unmixed motives. We consider how our words will be received and our reputation shaped before we speak. We give generously and then expect our reward. We do nice things, anticipating favorable responses from those we help. The truth is that oftentimes what we most want is not the actual fruits of our efforts but to bask contentedly in the sunshine of our self-approval and to receive praise from others.

It is from this motive that many people bend to popular opinion, doing what they think will gain applause. While we do well in many instances to consider the wise counsel of others, winning their approval is not always clear gain. Countless lives have been diminished or squandered by actions aimed at gaining popularity instead of what better judgment would regard as wise. Oftentimes, popular thought is just plain wrong and judgments and actions aimed at winning praise from critics or the masses have proved to be disastrous. How often we hear of unpopular decisions that the masses once condemned but after history judged them proved to be prudent. What clamoring crowds once demanded be done has frequently, later on, been shown to be just plain wrong.

Selfish desires permeate most lives, and much of what we observe people doing reflects these appetites and ambitions. The trick to acting with integrity lies in one's honesty, particularly in being brutally honest with one's real desires and motives. Does one decide on the basis of what others think and say? Is the goal to please them and, thereby, to secure their approval? Or, does one make judgments independently of anticipated praise or blame? The ideal is to decide on the basis of what one honestly believes to be in the long-term best interests of all concerned. An illustration of this is brought out by the experience of David Kimball, who once was chairman and CEO of General Signal and, before that, president of Rohm & Haas Co. in Philadelphia. David told me about an incident that took place early in his career, when he ran a small company of five hundred employees that manufactured products for the military.

At the time, David's firm was competing aggressively for a large contract. And, it looked like his company was going to win it. The evaluation of their proposal had gone extremely well. There was just one "hitch," and it surfaced privately at the last minute. The procurement person from the firm that was about to place the order wanted something—a bribe! Of course it wasn't stated in those terms, but that's what it amounted to. Namely, he wanted a thousand dollar stereo, which was fairly extravagant at the time. David's company could purchase the stereo as a gesture of "thanks" for receiving the large order. What could a thing like this matter? It was a small sum in relation to the size of the order and no one would have to know about it. David Kimball didn't like the smell of proposition and he told the man, "No. We're not going to do that." The salesman who was handling the account for David's company said, "Well, we're going to lose this contract if we don't give him what he wants."

On the one hand, as David Kimball saw it, his company needed the business. If they didn't get the large order, they'd have to lay off sixty or seventy employees. That would be distasteful—and make him very unpopular. On the other hand, bribery was wrong. It certainly isn't a good basis on which to run a business. Beside that, David knew that dishonest dealings have a way of changing a person. After a while dishonesty twists a person into someone no one respects or wants to do business with. That would be distasteful, too. And, then how might the employees feel if they learned that they worked for an unethical firm? Dave weighed the matter fully. As it would for everyone else, this thing called temptation glittered brightly in his mind. David made his decision: he turned down the offer. He told his associates, "If it's going to take a payoff to get the contract, then we just don't want it."

Conquer What Destroys Character

As we have been saying, humans are social creatures—and we must never forget that. We are made for companionship and feel deprived without it. We want to feel loved, needed, and respected. The motives behind many of one's actions, perhaps most actions, can be traced to these desires. This is why most people are deeply concerned with their standing in the eyes of others, which has its benefits. The desire for a good reputation serves as a strong deterrent to unwanted behavior. But the need for approval can also become an obsession. And when it does, it can destroy peace of mind and the ability to choose wisely.

It's a fairly typical pattern for people to worry less and less about what others think about them as they age. With each passing year they realize more and more that such concern is not only a waste of time but something that lessens their enjoyment of life. John Steinbeck, the Nobel Prize–winning author, once recounted an experience he had as he was coming down from Sag Harbor, New York, on a train. Sitting in front of him was a young lady and her tweedy, pipe-smoking grandfather. All the way down the coast this young lady was talking her head off about other people and what they thought of her. When the train finally stopped in New York, the old man took a puff on his pipe and turned to the young lady and said, "You wouldn't worry so much about what people think of you if you realized how little they care."

No serious mind can admire choices or actions that come cheaply and at the expense of avoiding difficult thought or for the sheer purpose of winning the praises of others. When we think of it, we realize that deciding what to do is fairly simple when the decision-maker's sole concern involves what others think and what they will praise. But this approach does not guarantee sound choices. It is quite the opposite. Actions directed at gaining praise from others are not just dishonest but also generally less effective. We are better off being our true selves; we perform better when we do this. And when we do, others will see us as being authentic.

America's troubadour, Burl Ives, late in life once told an interviewer his experience with outgrowing the desire for approval: "The difference between me as a young man and me as an old man is all a matter of intent. Twenty years ago I liked to go to nightclubs in New York and have people come up to me and say, 'You're Burl Ives, the great performer.' Much of my earlier life was spent seeking that kind of external gratification. I went out in front of an audience with the idea that I'm going to put it over on the audience. I had a planned walk onto the stage, I had a planned set of songs, and I even planned what I was going to do with my face when I'd crack a joke and such. It was as well planned as a good bank robbery! Well, it was all contrived. Now I'm smart enough to know that the only time I can sing effectively is when I've got but one purpose, and that's to touch the hearts of as many people as I can" (www.burlives.com).

Those we most admire from the pages of history distinguished themselves largely because they neglected the changing and conflicting opinions of others. They faithfully followed their own standards, what their minds respected. Benjamin Franklin, that wise American whose sage advice shaped many minds, knew well the treachery of popular opinion. In a letter to his sister he wrote: "True happiness depends more upon one's own judgment of one's own self in acting properly and with the right motivations than upon the applause of the unthinking, undiscerning multitude, who are apt to praise him one day, and condemn him the next" (Smyth, 1907). We can condense these ideas into a simple statement of advice: Act on the basis of what you believe is right and not on what you think will earn praise or avoid blame. An honest person is not concerned with whether an action will be praised but with whether that action ought to be praised.

Integrity is doing what one believes to be right as his conscience so guides him. The ideal is to be unconcerned with winning the praises of others. In the *Apology*, Socrates advised, "A man who is good for anything ought not to calculate the chance of living or dying; he ought only to consider whether in doing anything he is doing right or wrong, acting the part of a good man or of a bad."

The greatness of Abraham Lincoln is revealed by his steadfast adherence to what he believed to be right and good for the nation, despite the bitter attacks against him in the press. In many ways he chose to make himself impervious to their criticism. When asked why he did not try to defend his actions, President Lincoln said that history would be a far better judge of him than contemporary critics. If he were to respond to every attack, he believed, it would not be possible for him to attend to the things that really required his attention.

Those driven to earn praise actually enslave themselves to the petty likes and dislikes of others. They cease being their own persons. What drives the praise seeker is not to be outstanding but to fit in. The moods and passing preferences of others are not the best guides to follow in deciding what to do and how to act. All too frequently this approach to life leads to profound confusion, dissatisfaction, and, ultimately, ruin. We are all familiar with others, so concerned with getting things, that they forget who they are. They sacrifice their dignity, their reputations, their honor, and their humanity to get what is, ultimately, not important.

The Angry Mob Phenomenon

As harmful as the pursuit of praise can be to good decision making, there is also its cousin, the "angry mob mentality," which is even more treacherous. This phenomenon occurs whenever a hate group develops to permanently quiet someone who says or does something that's threatening or unpopular. Like a lynch mob, people join in partly to fit in and partly to see their point of view prevail. And it is an ever-present possibility, particularly in an age when so many people go through life getting what they want by playing the role of victim and trying to destroy the reputation of someone else with false accusations.

We really need only a small sampling of life's experiences to tell us that not all people do get along. Indeed, we all have a tendency to rub someone else the wrong way. In any organization there is at least one person whom someone else would like to "put in his place" or dispose of altogether. The motives for this are legion. One way to do this is to charge the offensive party with the high crime of ethical misconduct. This is exactly what happened to an acquaintance of mine named Jim.

To be blunt about it, Jim is no saint. He isn't mean spirited or dishonest but he can be temperamental at times. He is known to come across to others as abrupt; but that's just Jim being Jim. On the positive side, he is a good worker and he is productive. Jim's boss sees him as an occasional nuisance, not because he is disruptive and uncooperative but because Jim's subordinates sometimes complain about the work he assigns them to do. Jim's boss just doesn't like to be bothered. While it would be incorrect to say that Jim and his boss dislike each other, it is also true that they do not like each other very much. At best, they tolerate each other. They have dealt with their differences by steering clear of one another as much as practical, which has worked out fairly well. But big trouble brewed for Jim from elsewhere in the organization.

Jim is a demanding boss himself. Let there be no mistake about that. He expects the best from those who work for him and he gets it. He isn't mean or underhanded, and he has never caused anyone any harm. He's just a bit abrupt with people from time to time when he's preoccupied with pressing matters. Regardless, he is thoroughly professional.

Things ran this way for a long time. Work was getting done; no one was getting hurt or terribly upset; things progressed satisfactorily. Yet, tensions existed. There were a few bumpy spots. Then, one day some of Jim's underlings got to talking among themselves. In fact, one of them had developed a vicious dislike for Jim. So, what amounted to being anti-Jim forces began gossiping among themselves. After a time the gossip intensified, each person found something bad to say about Jim. Each person, thinking himself or herself to be a victim, got to thinking that Jim was a source of their pain. And, as each person told twisted tales about Jim, that person felt that he or she grew a bit in stature in the minds of the others present.

At first the gossip was small stuff: Jim was this or that—all bad things, of course. But over time the tone and content of the gossip grew worse. After a while, Jim wasn't just a small nuisance any longer. He was a first-rate menace; something had to be done! One employee who had a particularly strong dislike for Jim finally announced a remedy: Jim must be disposed of and the sooner the better.

With that, the anti-Jim band began looking high and low for something, anything, that Jim might have said or done that could be used against him, to land Jim in hot water. This was not necessarily an organized effort at first; nonetheless, it evolved. Before long Jim's enemies began snooping into all phases of his life, hoping to find something on him. And, lo and behold, guess what? They found some dirt on him, because Jim is like everyone else—he's not 100% pure. The smell of his blood intensified their efforts. It wasn't long before the band of people who were out to destroy Jim told Jim's boss about what they had found out. This brought Jim's boss into helping the anti-Jim forces with their plot.

Jim's boss, already ill-disposed toward him, listened with great interest to what the group had to say. Rather than following the formally established procedures for airing grievances, which require complainants to go to their superiors first, Jim's boss listened and sided with the disgruntled employees. "We've got to get more information to build a case against him," Jim's boss told them. To this end the boss called Jim to his office and, without his knowledge of the inquiry, tricked the unsuspecting Jim into tattling on himself, revealing small misdeeds he—like practically everyone else—had committed off the job.

With everyone looking for flaws in Jim and keeping careful notes, the list of his misdeeds grew. Then, with these in hand, Jim's boss drew up formal charges of wrongdoing against Jim. Even though these charges were not specific violations of the organization's rules or ethics code, they appeared to have merit. Here's what the anti-Jim forces said he did wrong: (1) They felt the tax accounting methods he used in his small, sideline business were inappropriate. (2) Jim used an outdated computer program from work on his home computer, which was legal according to the license agreement with the software provider, but his accusers would not accept this legal point. (3) He got mad one day at work and yelled at an employee from another department who had gone to Jim's boss to complain about him. On the surface the charges made Jim out to be a very bad person who must be terminated immediately.

The "get-Jim" movement reached its peak when formal charges of wrongdoing were brought against Jim. Top leadership had no particular axe to grind with him. But as they saw it, the power structure had to be preserved and this meant supporting those lower down in the chain of command. Their view was that if his boss said Jim was guilty, then they'd go along with what the boss said. Besides, Jim is a "nobody." In truth, those at the top of the organization were more concerned with remaining popular with underlings than they were with truth and fairness. Upper-level management initiated disciplinary proceedings against Jim. Indeed, Jim was in "hot water" and no one had the courage to challenge the allegations. Like scared animals, everyone ran for cover. As they saw it, this was Jim's problem, not theirs.

Now what took place in the minds and actions of upper level management and Jim's co-workers was remarkable and frightening. These ordinarily decent folks somehow forgot that they were human themselves. They began to see themselves as judges. In their minds they perceived themselves to be a good bit purer than Jim. They got to looking at every scrap of evidence against Jim with moral outrage. This is what contempt can do to anyone. As they observed the situation from their perches of purity, the things Jim had done were unpardonable.

The truth is that accusations against Jim were over things little different than what others in the organization were doing themselves. But these others weren't unpopular with management, as Jim had now become. And everyone whispered to himself, "What's happening to Jim would never happen to me because I'm liked around here." Worse still, no one was the slightest bit concerned about the pain Jim was experiencing throughout his ordeal.

Jim was accused of many violations—not just one. Not one of them amounted to very much by itself but that wasn't the problem in the minds of those who were out to get him. It was the accumulation of many things that mattered—at least that's what they said to convince themselves of the rightness of what they were doing.

Now, some of the allegations against Jim had a small measure of truth to them. After all, Jim is no saint. What this amounted to was that those in power found fault with Jim, not because he had broken established rules but because he wasn't flawless.

Then one day, George, a courageous friend, saw what was going on and he stood tall, denouncing what the anti-Jim forces were doing. George didn't have a political agenda to distort his mind or heart. And he wasn't like the scared rabbit-like co-workers who ran for cover to protect themselves. George saw clearly the injustice, the shabby charges, the motivating political agenda, the unfairness of what was taking place. Ultimately, George persuaded those at the highest rungs of power to more or less see what had really gone on below— the witch hunt. George wasn't entirely successful, but at least he saved Jim from losing his job. The sad part was that those at the very top of the organization held to the thought that what they did was reasonable because Jim wasn't perfect. And this is the point—no one is "that" pure. The question George was unable to get those at the very top of the organization to address was as follows: How pure must one be to keep his or her job? And, if they do come up with a standard, then they darn well better state it plainly for everyone to see beforehand.

Accept What the Facts Suggest

Many years ago, when I worked for the Anaconda Company, a problem arose in our open-pit copper mine in Butte, Montana. Absenteeism had shot up. It was a troublesome problem, particularly in view of the fact we were less efficient at producing copper than were our chief competitors.

A friend of mine, Don Roach, was the industrial engineer there. It was his job to study problems like this and make suggestions for improving operations. Don went to work on the problem. He first collected all the information he could lay his hands on—numbers of employees, work records from payroll, time cards, etc. From these data, Don prepared a graph showing the number of absences per shift over a period of thirteen months. His graph revealed a sudden upturn. Naturally, there were "spikes" in absenteeism—a few days when the absences shot way up but fell back down later. These could easily be explained: the first few days of hunting season, the first day of fishing season. These times always had more than the usual numbers of absences. Doesn't everyone's grandmother get sick on the opening day of baseball? But, these aberrations aside, there was a definite pattern. The average number of absences per shift had suddenly jumped up. In fact it had nearly doubled and it held there, steady. What could account for this? Don searched for an explanation.

What Don discovered was that work schedules for operators in the Berkeley Pit, the open-pit mine, were changed. Whereas previously miners in the Berkeley Pit worked five shifts a week, they were now working six shifts a week. The timing of this work schedule change coincided with the upturn in absences. To Don, the answer was simple—the schedule change caused the absenteeism problem.

Now, you'd think that top management would welcome Don's fine work. Life is never so simple. They rejected what his data suggested, because top management didn't want to return to the five shifts per week schedule. That, they argued, wasn't the problem. The problem, as they saw it, was the employees. They were part of a new generation that had a strong distaste for hard work.

The Capacity to Accept Disagreement

Being one's own person and not being overly concerned with gaining popularity is not the same thing as ignoring the ideas and feelings of others. Very often there are to be found within any organization voices that ought to be heard and considered. Sometimes these voices are those of very unpopular people and the source of their unpopularity can well be caused by their willingness to speak out on issues that others view differently. Some of the finest managers I have ever known are inclined to give hospitable consideration to these contrary ideas expressed. Yet, there are many other managers who never get the benefit of an opinion other than their own. They never hear contrary views, which may be correct and useful. And when they do hear these opinions and ideas, they immediately move to hush them up. In too many organizations, popular opinion, accepted patterns of thought, and commonly held assumptions are never questioned or challenged. And whenever the popular mood is challenged with a contrary opinion, the person voicing it is labeled as odd or disloyal or just plain wrong or, worse yet, a troublemaker.

One outstanding quality of the best bosses is their willingness to listen to opposing ideas, different ideas, challenging ideas. These bosses encourage subordinates by hearing what they have to say and by acting on good ideas brought up. In the course of running his business, Paul Galvin, who started and ran Motorola for many years, managed to convince his associates that he was not infallible. They soon learned that they could go to him and say, "Paul, your decision yesterday was wrong." If the new facts they supplied stood the test of his scrutiny, he would accept their analysis. Some recall his words, "Tell the fellows we're changing. My decision yesterday was wrong." He pursued good, clear thinking and did not stand on his position or office, being too arrogant or proud to back down or accept other ideas. Results were what he was after. Galvin often said, "Follow the right decisions regardless of when, or how, or by whom these decisions were arrived at" (Petrakis, 1965). Here was a man who did not want to have people working for him who would not admit their own mistakes.

A person has to be of big enough caliber to accept disagreement and entertain diverse points of view. Tex Thornton, the driving force who pieced together the "Whiz Kids" for Ford Motor Company and later built Litton Industries into a large-scale enterprise, was one such person. He insisted on honest thinking. He even encouraged dissent from his inner circle of trusted associates. Thornton didn't allow "committee think." He demanded that everyone form and express his own opinions. Thornton said, "I once had a boss who made the wrong decision and I told him so. He said he judges the loyalty of subordinates by how well they carry out his wrong decisions. I judge employees by how well they tell me I'm wrong."

The "Sloan meetings," once held at General Motors serve as yet another illustration of a climate that is supportive of open debate and free inquiry. The words of Alfred P. Sloan to the GM board of directors capture the flavor of this climate. "Gentlemen," Sloan would say, "I take it we are all in complete agreement on the decision here. Then I propose we postpone further discussion of this matter until our next meeting to give ourselves time to develop disagreement and perhaps gain some understanding of what the decision is all about." An important idea behind these meetings, as Sloan explained, was this: "It is the right as well as the duty of every managerial employee to criticize a central management decision which he considers mistaken or ill-advised." Criticism was not just not penalized, it was encouraged, as a sign of initiative and an active interest in the business.

Help Someone by Unflattering Criticism

Contrary to common supposition, it's not always a good idea to be nice to people in ways that are entirely pleasing to them at the moment. Frequently our desire to be liked is the enemy of genuine helpfulness. While it is usually safe advice to not meddle in the lives of others, it is also worth one's while to consider the consequences of not doing so and what the true motives are behind our desires to act or not to act. If I have a friend who is doing something that I firmly believe is harmful to himself or herself, then, of course, I need to ask myself whether I ought to say something or keep quiet. I also should ask myself, "Why would I choose one course over the other one?" If I am remaining mum because I feel my friend's doings are his or her affairs and not mine, that's one thing. But suppose I conclude that my keeping mum is because either (1) I really don't care or (2) saying something might cause my friend to dislike me. Both of these reasons have a selfish motivation to them. Sometimes helping someone requires displeasing them.

William Anderson, who once ran NCR, told me about a situation he faced. He had a senior-level man working under him. This other man did something that's entirely human: he fell madly in love with one of the secretaries. But he didn't stop there; he let his emotions lead him into doing something better judgment would advise against doing. He began pursuing her romantically. The problem was that the man was married and he had a family. An extramarital relationship that was beginning to blossom would surely spoil a happy and wholesome marriage. Soon, with his emotions out of control, the man started making a fool of himself by his silly, boyish behavior and others noticed it. So, Anderson called the man into his office and scolded him, and told him to cut it out. The man didn't like it, but he understood what his boss was telling him. A lesson to be gained from this story is that we do well to consider whether doing something is better than not doing anything at all. One way of answering this question is to be dead honest with ourselves regarding our underlying motives. It is useful to realize that for the sake of temporarily pleasing someone we might leave that person permanently worse.

Procter & Gamble chairman and CEO A. G. Lafley told *Fortune* ("The Best Advice I Ever Got," Mar. 21, 2005), that the most influential person in his life was his mother. Described as a strong, proud Irish woman, she advised her son to be independent, to be himself. Years later and in his sixth year at P&G, Lafley decided he'd quit his job and go to work at a high-powered consulting firm in the east. He didn't like the stifling bureaucracy at P&G and change there was slow. Lafley handed his resignation letter to his boss, who read it and then proceeded to tear it up right in front of him. He told his boss, "I made a copy." His boss told him to go home and to call him that night. When Lafley called him, his boss told him to not come into the office for the next week but to come by the boss's house every night so the two men could talk. In the relaxation of his boss's home, Lafley finally opened up to what was eating at him. The problem with P&G was the bureaucracy. His boss said, "You're running away. You don't have the guts to stay and change it. You'll run away from your next job too." It was tough language but not tougher than Lafley himself. He decided to stay and fight. He would later set his ambition to changing things and speaking up every time something didn't work. And, as he continued to be his own person and speaking up, he kept getting promoted—all the way to the very top.

Rise above the Pursuit of Popularity

Here are some of the main ideas we discussed in this chapter:

1. Evaluate your motives before taking action. Are you pursuing what is praiseworthy or what will earn you praise?
2. Avoid going along with the crowd in what's known as "groupthink."
3. Face the facts about situations honestly. Put facts and logic and the conclusions they lead to ahead of accepted patterns of beliefs.
4. Learn to accept disagreement. In fact, try to encourage some amount of it. Invite debate in the pursuit of better answers and solutions to problems.
5. When the time is right, go ahead and offer your opinions if they are honestly aimed at helping someone.

CHAPTER 10

Use Good Judgment

Determine what's best overall in each situation and be decisive

A few years ago I met a man named John M. Griffin, who had just retired as Director of Engineering for the B-2 Stealth Bomber. He told me about a difficult decision that he faced a few years earlier in connection with this project. It occurred during this aircraft's initial test flight. Hundreds of people, working around the clock, prepared for the event. They tested and retested every part of the plane. Everything looked to be in perfect order. Finally, the day of the initial test flight arrived. The press was on hand, as were generals and admirals and other high-ranking officers from the military. Members of Congress and presidents of companies that had contracts with the military were also present. The B-2 bomber taxied into position at the end of the runway. Then, the unexpected arose. As the pilot revved up the plane's engines, the on-board computer signaled a malfunction. It switched the main fuel feed to the backup system. John Griffin, watching the technical data being reported, realized that human judgment was needed immediately—his judgment. He had to decide, on the spot, what to do. Should he choose to please the assembled audience with the scheduled test flight and risk failure, or should he call an immediate halt to the mission? John had already rehearsed in his mind what he'd do under every conceivable situation and this situation told him "Stop." John wasn't going to allow the test pilot to risk his life just to please an expectant crowd. He decided that whatever had caused the computer controls to signal trouble must be identified and fixed first. The initial test flight would have to wait.

Making well-informed, solidly reasoned decisions is not a simple matter. It requires accurate information, sound logic, and good judgment. Oftentimes, there are pressures at play, working to push the decision maker in one way or another but not always in the smartest direction. While textbook logic tells us that decision makers should ferret out relevant information and evaluate the available evidence fairly, the process of making sound choices isn't as easy as all that. Whatever the decision is, in the end, judgment comes into play and it's this thing called judgment that deserves our special consideration. Judgment involves the ability to see all sides and all angles in a situation and to honestly consider the long-term consequences of each option. This is why integrity is so important. It enables us to be dead honest with the facts and evidence we observe and with our wants and feelings and prejudices.

One of the more difficult aspects of making sound decisions involves questioning commonly accepted assumptions about the situation at hand that are crucial to effective analysis. All too often we find commonly held suppositions to be based on other people's claims instead of hard evidence that has been carefully scrutinized. A newspaper reports someone's opinion as if it were entirely true, and others read that report and accept the statements by the person quoted. "It was in the newspaper," a person says, "it must be true." Good judgment sees through this shallow thinking and demands firm evidence before forming opinions about the nature of any situation. All too often we want so much to believe things that we fail to question the basis on which we hold our opinions. Honest thinking always questions assumptions and demands solid evidence. It is little swayed by the say-so of unknown persons.

Deciding When Every Option Has Flaws

Integrity helps us try our level best to choose wisely, especially when every available option is flawed. Here's an example of what I'm talking about. Several years ago I was in Peoria, Illinois, and visited George Schaefer, who headed up the Caterpillar Tractor Company at the time. He told me about an experience that he once had, years before, when he managed a factory. It required good judgment.

One Monday morning, just as he arrived for work, George faced a decision, and it was a tough one. What made matters worse was that members of his staff were hotly divided over how the situation should be handled. It all began when a factory employee had driven up to the plant's gate in his pickup truck over the weekend. The truck was loaded with Caterpillar parts and tools, which the employee had pilfered over many years. The man's misdeeds had begun to bother him; his conscience couldn't take it any longer. So, he decided to return what he had stolen and make a full confession. What should be done with him?

George had to decide. The labor relations people and the head of the accounting department said, "He's reformed. Scold the man and give him a mild punishment.

But don't fire him. Keep him on the payroll. He has a good work record, otherwise." The head of manufacturing and the quality control and engineering people advised just the opposite. "Wrong is wrong," they argued. "The company has rules. He stole from us and he should be terminated! We need to make an example of him so others don't steal."

George listened to all sides, weighing the matter from every conceivable angle before deciding. There were so many factors to consider: What would be best for the company and best for the man? Now the man was a thief all right. There wasn't any doubt about that. He had stolen from the company. But he had come forward and confessed. While it was true that he had "thieving" qualities, it was also true that he had other qualities, too, namely the willingness to confess. This situation wasn't exactly the same thing as catching someone in the act of stealing and lying about it. So, George thought through the possible implications of each option: If we punish this man, what's that going to say to other employees? Maybe others have stolen and would like to confess; it could open our eyes to security slip-ups or to hidden morale problems. What will the union say in this matter? Should we be unbendingly tough, or does this case merit compassion?

Questions and concerns such as these traveled through George's mind as he pondered what to do. He studied every scrap of pertinent information he could get. And he listened to his key lieutenants as they expressed their opinions. George wanted to make a fully informed and well-reasoned decision. He was thinking and deciding with integrity, being totally honest with the facts and himself. Then George decided. It was what he considered the best thing to do on balance. He sent the employee back to work with a stern warning that if he ever stole again, it would cost him his job. That was George's judgment.

The Reality of Right and Wrong

In many minds it has become convenient to look at the world in relative terms— that what is right in one situation might not be right in another situation. This idea, as correct as it might be in many cases, has invited the attitude that "what is right for you may not be right for me." This is what we call *relativism*, the belief that right and wrong are merely a matter of opinion and that one person's opinion is just as good as anyone else's opinion. If carried to its logical conclusion, this argument says that there is really no such thing as right and wrong, a viewpoint that is contrary to what most people regard as common sense. The wise person sees integrity as being something that involves holding fast to the belief that right and wrong are not just a matter of one's opinion. To these people right and wrong do exist, regardless of whether we know what right and wrong are in any given situation. What makes something right or wrong, they believe, does not depend on the circumstances and it does not rest on opinion. Socrates, that wise old Greek philosopher, was thinking along these lines when he said, "There is a real and objective right, wholly independent of our opinions and wishes, which it is our whole duty to try to discover."

There is evidence aplenty from everyday life to convince us of the reality of right and wrong and dispel the myth of relativism. Consider the squabbles between people that you hear: "Hey, stop making so much noise. Don't you know that you're not supposed to be noisy in a library?" "You can't butt ahead of everyone else in line. You'll have to wait your turn, just like everyone else." "That isn't what you promised you'd deliver. I'm not paying for it."

What's interesting about conflict is that you do not merely hear that one person's behavior displeases another person. You also hear that each person in the argument has in mind a rule of how the world ought to be run and that the other party has violated it. Time and again the justification each one uses to present his side of the argument is based on the idea that the other person has broken a rule—that the offending party did something that should not be done. I think this shows us that everyone, even the most hardened criminal, believes that universal standards of right and wrong exist, regardless of whether we know what they are. I also think this illustration suggests that even the worst elements of our race would prefer an ordered world structured on right and wrong to a disordered world that is not.

Another piece of evidence that can raise our level of certitude that right and wrong exist, comes from an experience that Christina Hoff Sommers once related. At the time of this incident, Professor Sommers was teaching philosophy at Clark University. For a long time she had a running debate with one of her colleagues. This colleague had been arguing that morality is relative—that right and wrong are a matter of opinion. Professor Sommers held the opposite view—that some things are right and others are wrong. One day Professor Sommers encountered her colleague, who was quite angry. "What's the problem?" Sommers inquired. "It's the students," her colleague replied. "I just looked at their term papers. They plagiarized." She was angry because the students had broken a rule—a rule that she honored.

The point to be made from this experience is that some things are clearly wrong. Lying is wrong. Stealing is wrong. Cheating is wrong. Being a nuisance is wrong. Other things are right. Telling the truth is right. Being kind is right. Giving your best effort is right. Playing fair and by the rules is right.

Several years ago I spent a day with a man named Bill Huessong. Bill was vice president of manufacturing for Shopsmith, Inc., in Dayton, Ohio, at the time. Many are familiar with the Shopsmith name. The company makes a five-in-one power woodworking tool. Bill told me something very important about this company's president, John Folkerth. He said, "With John, there isn't any room for gray in matters of right and wrong. To him, it's either black or white; they are either right or wrong."

Now this is not to say that he thought any choice or any action was either all right or all wrong. Of course he could see that there could be right and wrong in any choice or action. But what was significant here was that Mr. Folkerth saw the existence of right and wrong. As a consequence, everyone who worked for John knew that certain things would be tolerated and other things would not. This climate served to give everyone at Shopsmith a clear understanding of what were the boundaries of acceptable behavior.

Here is an illustration of how he got his message across to employees. John Folkerth once learned that a few people in his organization had installed a computer software program on more than one of the company's computers. They had bought one copy of the software and, in violation of the copyright agreement, had installed it on more than one computer. John Folkerth found out about it and told them what they had done was wrong. He had his purchasing department pay the software publisher for what they were using, just as the agreement stipulated. One of the people who had been involved offered up the excuse, "But that's what everyone else does." Folkerth was unimpressed and unmoved. He told the employee, "We don't do that here. We pay for what we use." It wasn't something that could be excused.

Calling right and wrong "a matter of opinion" is really quite foolish when you come to think of it. For one thing, it affords us with a handy excuse to do anything we might feel like doing. It is an easy way out to escape blame. For another thing, it blinds us to a full and honest assessment of the issues we consider as we contemplate options. And, it allows us to excuse ourselves for any undesirable action we might take. And if we can excuse ourselves after harming our neighbors, then, by the same logic, they ought to be able to do the same thing to us.

The Highest Form of Judgment Is Required Whenever Each Option Has Some Negative Aspect

The ideal approach to decision making considers all the costs and benefits, all the pros and cons, all the positive and negative implications of each option. And it involves choosing in ways that advance the embodiment of ideals. How different this approach is from what happens when we face real-life situations and make decisions. In so many of the situations we find ourselves, there is no flawless path. Everything we might choose to do will contain some unlikable or unsavory dimension, albeit quite small. This is the nature of the world in which we live. So, while we might not be able to avoid doing some amount of wrong—hopefully, a very tiny amount—we can still do some amount of good. Highly regarded people who make difficult decisions every day sleep well at night because they realize that while they might not be able to lead flawless lives, they can still lead useful lives.

Consider the situation that a CEO of one of our country's largest aluminum companies once faced. He had to decide what to do when no flawless option existed. The problem he faced involved an aluminum smelter located in a foreign country. The smelter employed local labor, many were uneducated. By today's standards the smelter was outmoded technologically, but it was still earning a respectable profit. Owing to the nature of the old technology at the smelter, tar fumes were being released. They are not harmful in minute concentrations, but they are a hazard to those working there over extended periods. Tar fumes are a known carcinogen. These tar fumes can be collected by means of a roof monitor system, which is how modern plants are constructed, but that would be cost prohibitive in this situation. However, company engineers created a way around the danger—cool hats. Cool hats are self-enclosed fresh air systems that are to be worn at all times by employees working at the smelter.

Now, this plant was making a profit. It was a good employer in the region and did not present a health hazard as long as employees wore the protective equipment provided. But they didn't always do that, despite rules and warnings and constant supervision. Regardless of the tremendous effort that went into educating these employees and monitoring their behavior, they preferred to remove their cool hats complaining that they were "uncomfortable." Now, the question: Should the company close down the smelter or keep it opened?

This really wasn't an easy question. Neither option was desirable. On the one hand, there was the economic health of the local community. Income was vitally important to people who had families to feed and house and clothe. On the other hand, there was the matter of the very real possibility that money-desperate employees might ignore company safety rules and expose themselves to cancer-causing fumes.

Levels of Thinking in Decision Making

How deep the difference is between the immature person and the mature person. The childish thoughts and concerns of the immature person center on self, with all its changing wants. And like dry leaves drawn up into the autumn sky by a whirlwind moving across a recently harvested cornfield, these wants and concerns flutter about. At the simplest level of thinking, at the immature level, one arrives at decisions by considering the benefits that come to self from each choice. And so, as people at this level of thinking contemplate their options, they consider how each one would impact their convenience, their likes and wants, their own interests, their personal agenda, their reputation. Their chief concern, and hence criterion for deciding, is self. What these people most need to learn is that such a childish outlook works against them. Its inconsistencies in concerns, its obvious self-seeking nature, and its logical fallacies when gauged against larger concerns make impossible any consistent pattern of choice and, hence, any respect for the person who operates in this way.

Maturity involves expanding one's concerns beyond self to include the interests, wants, and well-being of others. The ideal is to be impartial to one's own interests and the interests of others. The more mature individual respects the values and standards that protect civilization and serve to better the human condition. The nature of thinking at this level considers decision options in light of society's standards—its rules, laws, and codes of conduct. The reasoning involved at this level of thinking is pretty basic. One uses time-tested rules of right and wrong in making difficult choices. But life is rarely so easy. Complex decisions are always nested in complex circumstances with troublesome complications to be considered. Each available option has some disturbing side effect to it and each one violates one rule or another. Then what should be done?

The most fully developed mind moves ahead in life purposefully, with the conviction that the only lasting certainty we have is that humans are best off when they live by ideals, when ideals are the guiding standards by which choices are made. These decision makers are driven by the persistent desire for these ideals to permeate every life, every situation. These people make decisions by first gauging the impact each option has on promoting these ideals. This is tricky, because in many cases—if not all cases—each option available works both for and against one or more of these ideals. The mature mind realizes that judgment is always needed and it must be preceded with honest reflection and a commitment to do what's best overall. That's the ideal path; but it is rarely followed perfectly. Few, if any, of us are altruistic enough to put these ideals ahead of ourselves.

There is always the tendency for a person to do whatever it takes to get what's wanted, to pursue what most benefits self, and then to justify that decision with an idealistic-sounding reason. And so, a person looks at a situation that calls for a decision, chooses that which promises the most benefits for self-gain, and then thinks of how that choice advances a worthy ideal, so as to be able to explain the choice to others in nice-sounding terms. This is a common form of dishonesty—choosing that which is primarily self-enriching and then thinking of ways to make that selfish decision appear noble. It requires an enormous amount of honesty for a person to be able to rise above this temptation. Those who succeed at this begin by admitting to themselves that the temptation is real and that they are vulnerable to it. That done, they next turn to a time-tested approach to living that has proved to be effective in removing self as an end.

The basic fact about humans that we need to understand is that something is always dominating their desires. It can be self or others or a great cause; but it will always be something. Those who have demonstrated the greatest capacity to remove themselves as their first concern have succeeded because they deliberately chose to serve something far greater, far more important, and far more enduring than self. These people are reverent to something they believe is supreme and sacred. And they serve it faithfully. By so doing, they subordinate their wants, their comfort, their pride, and their enrichment to something they feel is more important.

But this mind set is not easily attained. And when it is reached, it is always accompanied by some degree of pride, with all of its destructive possibilities. Because humans are always aware of what they are doing, it is impossible for them to escape a feeling of smugness that always accompanies high-minded ways. Anyone who consciously tries to remove self from the center of concern and then tries to replace it with something else inevitably reintroduces a new version of self back into his or her center of concern. This reintroduced version of self cannot help but see itself as being self-sacrificing, nobler, far better than anyone else. It is a prideful self that's arrogantly critical of all others who are not as "selfless."

How different our world would be if decision makers were able to replace concern for self with a greater concern, a concern for something else, and to not think about self at all. This would be much like what happens when a mother or father gives up her or his own welfare or safety for the good of a child they deeply love, a child they care more about than they do about their own well-being.

Deciding What Is "Best" Overall

A guiding principle of any sound system of ethics is the honest acceptance of something known as "comparative difficulties." This involves rising above naïve thinking by recognizing that ours is a complex world where no perfect choices exist. Simplistic, single-concern solutions are always inadequate. Intellectual honesty forces us to admit that there are enormous difficulties associated with every option. While we are morally obligated, of course, to think creatively and formulate every conceivable option when facing difficult choices, we are also morally obliged to act before conditions worsen and thereby present us with options that are worse still. Our experience tells us that whatever the situation and whatever the available options, each possible course of action will contain some undesirable element. We do not live in a utopia. This is the human predicament: evils are found everywhere, even in "good" solutions. The examples of this truth are ever present: While it may be wrong to pollute the air, it is even more wrong to allow people to freeze by not having heat. I can spend my time doing good for one cause, but that choice prevents me from doing some other kind of good for another cause.

One of the most sophisticated ethical truths is that the "best" and the "least evil" option are one in the same. Wisdom lies not in rejecting a course of action because it is not ideal but in the honest comparison of every conceivable, practical possibility. In our imperfect world; the best is never the ideal best. It is clearly wrong to select a greater evil than a lesser one. But it is also clearly wrong to not decide when indecision—which is a decision itself—is worse than pursuing another, less-flawed course. This may not be the way we would like it to be, but it is the way things are.

Many years ago, a large American chemical company with a plant in Mexico found itself in a tough spot, without an easy answer. Because of a broken pump and no replacements available within the country, the Mexican plant was forced to shut down. The pressures involved in the chemical processes and the operating requirements demanded a special type of pump. And the one they had was now broken. New parts to repair the pump would have to be brought into the country, because none were available in Mexico.

This plant was vitally important to the economic life in the area. It employed over five hundred people. What's more, Mexico needed the agricultural product the plant produced—the fertilizers and related chemicals. It was Mexico's only source of these products. So, employees would be without work until the breakdown was corrected. Under ordinary circumstances, this breakdown posed little in the way of technical difficulties. The new parts could be sent via air freight to the location immediately and installed within a couple of days after that. The plant might be closed down for a few days, but employees could be put to work on other tasks that had been postponed. With some buildup in inventories, the product from the plant would continue to be available for the Mexican market but not for long. So, the new parts were shipped right away.

Unfortunately, once arriving in Mexico the speedy movement of replacement parts stopped. They were to go no farther until they cleared customs. Now there were two ways for the parts to get passed through customs. There was the slow way, which involved lots of paperwork and would take two to four months. Official government forms have a nasty habit of sitting on officials' desks unless there is an incentive. Yes, the Mexican customs agents wanted something for their trouble. It was their way of "encouraging" those who wanted the replacement parts to use the other way of getting parts through customs.

The other way for getting the parts through customs in Mexico involved what's known as a facilitating payment. This is something that motivates customs agents to act on what the payer wants done. In this case the agents felt that $500 was an appropriate amount for their trouble. Once paid, the parts would pass through customs and be sent on their way immediately. The entire process would take only a few minutes. Which option ought the chemical company to choose? Neither one was entirely desirable.

On the one hand, it's unlawful for U.S. companies to pay bribes. Besides that, doing so feeds an element of corruption. On the other hand, if the company chose not to take the expedient route, to not make the facilitating payment, the plant would close down for two to four months, maybe longer. All the while, the employees and the economy of the local community would suffer. And, too, there was the loss of product. It would not be available to the thousands of Mexican farmers who depended on it. Without this product, their crop yields would be diminished. What should the chemical company do?

In relying on rules and principles for making decisions, we must first recognize that we are placing trust in ideas that generally work but that are, not unlike ourselves, imperfect. They are, after all, the products of thought by imperfect creatures. Sometimes situations arise in which the full application of one principle conflicts with other principles or with the welfare of other people. Do we respect a principle or persons? And if we find the full application of one principle at conflict with another one, which path ought we choose?

Those who believe that there are simple answers to such questions are demonstrating their failure to understand the true complexities of moral situations and perhaps also their lack of compassion for other persons. When we think about it, there are reasons for principles and those reason are invariably grounded in the betterment of people. For instance, the ultimate reason for our keeping of promises is a respect for persons. Strict moralists—those who are concerned only with acting perfectly ethically themselves, never deviating from their standards—are frequently impervious to the suffering caused by unbending application of their principles. It takes a certain kind of self-righteousness for one to be more concerned with abstract principles than with persons. And so, their unbending reliance on rules works as an opiate to deaden whatever unease may remain within the submerged depths of their conscience. It should become evident from this discussion that the noblest principle is that there is something more precious than principles.

Using Judgment

Let's review the main ideas found in this chapter:

1. Realize that every option will have some negative aspect to it, some ethical flaw.

2. Yes, right and wrong do exist. They exist independently of what you or anyone else believes or wants.

3. Acknowledge openly all the good and bad aspects you can see in each option.

4. Try to get the notion of "what's in this for me?" out of your head.

5. As you face decisions, hold up ideals as standards against which you gauge each option.

6. The highest principle is that there is something more precious than principles. It is people.

CHAPTER 11

Face Difficulties Head-on

Respond to adversity and setbacks with positive actions

As we wind our way through life, with all its twists and bends, each of us, at one time or another, will find ourselves whipped and scratched, broken and weakened, flat on our back. It hurts and we don't like it. We get mad and we want to get even. We feel pain and we ask, "Why me?" We hurt on the outside and on the inside, and we want sympathy. But our noisy, angry world is already too busy with difficulties of its own to hear our cries or stop to help. So, we are thrown back on ourselves, left on our own and alone, to do what we can or will. And, so now we must respond. The question is, "How?"

There is no truer measure of the resilience of a human's spirit than the way that person behaves when ill fortune strikes. How does one deal with a long period of disappointment and failure? Here is where we see the real proof of one's character. Achievements and good fortune are always welcomed and graciousness and modesty are within most people's grasp when times are generous. But taking a beating and coming up smiling and fighting on—like having your mainsail ripped to shreds by high gusts and using all your imagination and strength to rig another sheet and sail on—this reveals one's true character. Life tests each of us. It sometimes puts us in situations and asks us, "What will you do?" But more often it places us in prolonged trials and asks us, "How much can you endure?" Do we hold fast to our wits, courage, and optimism and go on, or do we go to pieces?

What ought one to do when a break or setback occurs? How can honesty be of any use to us in situations like these? History bears powerful testimony to what works and what doesn't, to what renews and brings success, and what allows small defeats to destroy one permanently. Honesty compels us to realize that doing nothing in the face of difficulties is a form of escapism, which invariably makes matters worse. The person who tries to escape his troubles—there are many forms of escape with which everyone is familiar—or focuses attention on oneself with pity, enfeebles his ability to act effectively. Positive action is what's most needed, both for achievement of desired accomplishments and for the strengthening and renewing of one's spirit. The best way to keep oneself sane and hopeful in trying times is purposeful action directed toward admirable ends.

The value of a positive outlook is not alone useful to the person facing difficulties. It is most usually useful to everyone in plain and good times, too, when one is actively pursuing healthy possibilities. It is indeed a fact that most work is better performed when people have a plan of action to go by. Plans are logical. They are products of the mind. But there is something else even more important to success than a good plan. And, like a logical plan, this, too, needs to be prepared before work begins. Just as one forms a logical plan for the work to be done, one also needs to form the right convictions to implement the plan in the face of all the obstacles and complications that will surely arise. I am speaking here about an emotional dimension within those who carry out the plan: to be strong and hold an enthusiastic belief in a brighter future, to have a stout will to persevere, and to have a quick imagination to create ways of accomplishing the impossible when failure looms large. These are products of the heart and they ought to be created alongside the logical plan and before any undertaking begins. To produce at your best, choose to approach what you do positively.

Refuse to Be Defeated

The roster of the world's great persons is packed with examples of the will to face difficulties head on. During a performance of *Don Quixote* at the Sydney Opera House one night, Mikhail Baryshnikov performed a *grande jeté* across the stage. He landed badly and felt his left ankle turn under. "I could hear the bones crushing," he later told *People* magazine. The pain was excruciating. Yet, incredibly, he danced on right up to the final curtain. Dancing through injuries is what professionals do. They don't allow themselves even a grimace from their pain to spoil the illusion they wish to create on stage. Skillfully, Mikhail improvised a step to keep going. By reversing direction of a series of pirouettes, he was able to shift his weight onto his right leg. Then, at last, when the curtain fell, he collapsed to the floor in a dead faint.

This, in example, is the mark of a triumphant spirit—finishing the performance after a break has come. Nothing is so impressive as having the grit to keep moving ahead. This means getting on with life with what remains after a setback.

It means fighting with a scabbard after the sword is gone. And, it means battling on to win instead of nursing one's battlefield wounds.

At one point or another some calamity or setback befalls every life. A person's abilities may be diminished. Sight, alertness, strength, stamina, health—these may be lessened or wiped away altogether. Now what? Will the person struggle bravely and go on? Or, will the person complain, demand sympathy, and retreat into a world of hurt? It all depends on what the person is made of on the inside. Many of those whom we most admire have achieved magnificently because of their reservoir of inner strength. How else can we explain the will to continue found in people like Robert Louis Stevenson, who, although bedridden and nearly going blind and confined to a darkened room, wrote some of the greatest works of literature? What was there in a man like Beethoven, who, although deaf, wrote the most moving compositions the music world has ever known? While we may be limited in our scientific understanding of the work of Steven Hawking, the Englishman called the most remarkable scientist of our time, who gave us theories of black holes, quasars, and quarks to explain the cosmos, each of us, whether learned or simple, is unbounded in admiration for him. By an act of sheer will he shrugged off his paralysis and turned it from an infirmity into an advantage for long hours of concentration on questions and purposes he considers important. This is positive living, turning thoughts away from defeatism and refocusing them on conquering adversity.

The greatness of the human spirit lies in the will to do, to try to succeed by being brave, determined, resourceful. In the face of adversity and with bleak prospects for an agreeable outcome, the human spirit has, in countless situations, shown itself able to rise to the challenges at hand. Lifted by the power of their faith that a venture will succeed, that an answer will be found, that a brighter future lies ahead, humans surmount seemingly impossible obstacles. The secret of those whom we most admire is their unshakable enthusiasm to triumph, even in the midst of disaster and tragedy.

In a 1973 championship fight in San Diego, Muhammad Ali fought on after suffering a broken jaw at the hands of Ken Norton, only to lose by decision. Kirk Gibson of the Dodgers, barely able to walk from the pain of injured legs, stepped into the batter's box as a pinch hitter in a 1988 World Series game with two outs and men on base, and hit the ball out of the park to drive in the winning run. These are examples of positive spirits at their finest.

Transform Tragedy into Triumph

It seems to be a rule of life that no sooner does one door slam shut in our face than another one opens up. During the years leading up to World War II, there was a young French naval officer who searched for adventure. His enthusiasm led him to enter the fleet aviation academy at Hourtin, an Atlantic Coast town west of Bordeaux. A great war was once again approaching and people foresaw its terrible arrival and they worried. Still, this young officer's interests were stirred by speed and excitement like flying airplanes, driving cars—and women. And so, living wildly, one foggy night in 1936, his car's headlights failed, causing him to misjudge the road as he drove through the dark. Traveling at a high rate of speed, he came to a hairpin curve too tight to negotiate safely. His car left the road and, he inside, it rolled over several times.

Hours later and barely alive, the young man regained consciousness. He was losing blood and he thought he'd surely die. But help arrived. The accident crushed several ribs and perforated his lungs. Broken bones in his left forearm stuck through the skin. Doctors thought amputation was the best course because of massive nerve damage and the likelihood of infection. The young officer flatly refused. He underwent therapy for eight months. Finally, after much painful struggle, he willed himself to move one finger. It was a start. Many more months passed before he regained control of all his fingers. The young officer saw his ordeal as a test. Every morning, as he recalled years later, he'd wonder how lucky he was to be alive. The automobile crash, perhaps, saved him from entering the war—a war that took the life of every other cadet in his flying class.

The Navy sent this 26-year-old officer to Toulon on the Mediterranean coast, where he met Philippe Tailliez, a navy lieutenant. Tailliez encouraged the young man to swim in the sea to strengthen his arm, which he did. One summer's day Tailliez handed the young officer a pair of goggles and, using them for the first time, his eyes were opened to the world beneath the surface of the sea. It was then, swimming below the water's surface, that the young French naval officer, Jacques Cousteau, witnessed a new world of fish and undersea flora for the first time.

One outstanding distinction of those who overcame hardship and moved on to great success is the will to concentrate on getting full use from their abilities, doing well with whatever strengths they did have. The secret to the positive person is the ability to focus on the right things and to not be disheartened by the fact that other powers and possibilities are beyond their grasp. These are the people who grow large in ways they can grow. They do not become bitter and stymied by their limitations.

Many people have demonstrated this ability in various ways. Two important events took place in the life of Itzhak Perlman when he was only 4 years old: he was struck down with polio and was lifted up when he heard a recording of Jascha Heifetz. One event was a life-crippling blow; the other one was an inspiring standard. The first event would have subdued a less forceful boy. But young Itzhak chose to transform his life heroically by focusing his special talents on what he heard. And he grew to become one of the truly great violinists because of it.

This incident suggests the importance of giving our best to what matters most, to what will grow large and add meaningfully to ourselves and the lives of others. The lesson to be gained here is, knowing what to say "yes" to and what to ignore altogether. Jazz great Ray Charles captured this important idea when he said, "My eyes are my handicap, but my ears are my opportunity." That's the secret: It is saying "yes" to big things—things that build ourselves and add to the world positively—and saying "no" to those things that do not.

Cleanse Yourself of Sour Feelings

One of the most liberating concepts we can apply to our daily lives is that of ridding our hearts of bitterness. Perhaps you have become troubled by an unpleasant situation or by a hurtful, mean-spirited person. Maybe you have gotten into nasty encounters with this person. Of course, the most tempting thing to do is to fight back, to try to even the score. I have read numerous accounts of the corrosive effects of bitterness on the human mind and physical health. How can you rise above bitterness? The secret lies in cleansing yourself of all sour feelings. The best way to do that is to deliberately apply your attention toward productive pursuits, away from the source of conflict. By an act of will, avoid battle with this adversary. Do something nice for this person. The act of forgiveness is one of the most powerful forces for healing a person's inside that we know about. If you can do that, you will escape negativism and free yourself to do vastly more constructive things. Your mental state will improve, making you more productive, and you will become a far more pleasant person in the company of others.

As an illustration of what this can involve, let me tell you about a man named Frank Considine. Frank ran the National Can Company, located just outside of Chicago. When he was a young man starting out, higher-ups in his organization spotted his remarkable abilities. They moved him ahead, perhaps a little faster than he should have been advanced. Out of jealousy, one of Frank's contemporaries became envious and developed a dislike for him. It grew to the point that this other man was passing around to others unkind and untrue remarks about Frank. Now what Frank did was quite wise and positive—and it eventually worked out for the betterment of himself and the other man.

Frank chose to ignore the pettiness and the politics that the other man was using against him. He said to himself, "I'm not going to let this bother me," even though it did at the time. Francis Bacon (British essayist, 1561–1624) wrote an essay, *On Revenge*, which contained something that's terribly useful to keep in mind at times like the one Frank experienced. Bacon asked: "Why should I hate a man for loving himself more than me?" This thought puts a problem like the one Frank Considine faced in the proper perspective. It is also a useful thought for stopping one from doing foolish and harmful things.

By focusing his thoughts on productive pursuits and by saying to himself, "I'm going to do the right thing. I'm not going to change my method of operation," Frank got on with what was vastly more important than petty squabbles—the work of his company. And his superiors recognized his exceptional performance. But through his approach, Frank also won something else far greater. Eventually, because Frank refused to fight back, the other man outgrew his hostility and began to admire Frank for his courage and high principles. After a couple of years, the other man became big-minded enough to admit to himself that his jealousy was wrong. Eventually, he and Frank grew to become very good friends.

The ability to turn away from disappointment and then to direct one's best efforts toward productive pursuits can bring astounding results. Many years ago, where I live, a woman by the name of Pat Gifford moved to town with her husband and two children. Her husband, Jack, began his teaching career in our university's department of marketing. Pat thought she'd like to teach, too, and, because she had an advanced degree in textiles, she landed a position in the university's department of home economics. In that role Pat's teaching was good but her scholarly publications didn't meet her tenure committee's expectations and they denied her tenure. Now this sort of blow would have probably crippled most other people's spirit. And, in all honesty, Pat's feelings were hurt by it. But she wasn't the kind of person to be destroyed by disappointment. She certainly wasn't about to fume and fret and stew inside with bitterness. Instead, she moved on, looking for something else suitable to her interests and abilities—and they were extraordinary.

Shortly afterward, a job opened with a locally owned department store chain in nearby Dayton. Pat applied for the position and they hired her. Her job was to set up and conduct employee training. This work matched her interests and abilities. And Pat's fine work was soon recognized and appreciated by top management. Superiors also noticed something else, something rare. It was exactly what they needed for their growing enterprise—her positive, friendly attitude. Everyone liked Pat and everyone saw what a fine job she was doing. Because she was not one to hold bitterness in her heart, she was able to take in stride setbacks that come to every job. And she was more productive because of it. She rose above little things in which others would get themselves hopelessly tangled, and she ignored the pestering matters that so frequently sap one's best efforts. Advancement after advancement followed. She rose to the position of vice president of human resources of Elder Beerman, a chain of department stores with 335 locations in nine states.

How to Respond to Setbacks

Mary Kay Ash is among the great success stories of American business. She turned the disappointments in her life, which would have easily destroyed others, into high purposes. Mary Kay responded positively, using her disappointments and troubles as ideas and her motivation for building something useful. For it was because of her life's experiences—as troubling as they were—that she saw a need to be filled. She chose to do something instead of doing nothing.

Hers was not a life of ease and comfort, but it was rich with accomplishments. Before she turned 10, Mary Kay was given the responsibility of cooking, cleaning, and taking care of her invalid father while her mother worked. Mary Kay accepted responsibility and achieved well in school and sports. Her mother's words to her were, "You can do it." These words helped to build her sturdy self-confidence. This served her well when, in the Great Depression, Mary Kay's husband of 11 years deserted her, leaving her to support three children under the age of 8. She took a job with flexible hours selling Stanley Home Products, where she achieved great distinction. She went on to become national training director of another company, World Gift.

Tragedy struck in 1962, when Mary Kay's life and career were threatened by a rare paralysis on one side of her face. But, again, she rose above the adversity. Recovering from surgery, Mary Kay retired from World Gift. She was remarried by then, Mary Kay Ash, and living comfortably in Dallas, but she soon became bored. She decided to write a book on direct selling. As she wrote the book, it dawned on her that women had a terrible time in the business world. There were so many problems that they faced—working and keeping a family going.

So, Mary Kay made a list of what she saw was wrong with male-run companies and how they could be fixed so that working mothers could reach their top potential in business. This gave her an idea: she'd start her own company. It would hire the women she wanted to help. Her organization would be different—no sales quotas, flexible hours, few rules, and autonomy.

Ten years earlier Mary Kay had become acquainted with a woman who tried unsuccessfully to market her own line of skin creams. In 1963, Mary Kay purchased, for $500, the formulas for these products. In the years that followed, her marketing organization took form. She set up a nationwide network of independent sales representatives—they would be called beauty consultants. Mary Kay saw not so much a need for cosmetics as she did a desire in American women to feel good about themselves through earning added income and achieving recognition. Mary Kay hit upon a method—a very good method—to meet their needs and it evolved into a thriving enterprise: her skin care cosmetics business.

Here's the fascinating thing about Mary Kay's business. Her business wasn't skin creams and beauty care products. Mary Kay Ash was in the business of selling small businesses—small businesses women could run out of their homes. And this is what she did for thousands of women all across America.

Mary Kay's philosophy for running her firm was to market skin care products in a way that provided sales representatives with recognition and a sense of independence. Mary Kay sold her creams and other beauty aids to these women who, in turn, sold them to customers in their towns and neighborhoods. Unquestionably, the real factor behind Mary Kay's business success was her genius when it came to inspiring and recognizing her beauty consultants at meetings and annual conventions. These featured motivational speeches, sales incentives, and prizes like fur coats and pink Cadillac automobiles for the top performers. Mary Kay's "customers" were the independent businesswomen who sold Mary Kay Cosmetics. What Mary Kay Ash sold them is the chance to have a profitable business and to feel good about themselves through their effective performance followed by individual recognition.

Positive Outlooks Ignite Imagination

One important benefit of cultivating a positive approach is the inspiration it gives to the creative impulses of the mind. By a positive approach, I mean the dogged refusal to be defeated and an unending drive to take constructive action. Positive does not equate to feelings of contentment and happiness. Some of mankind's greatest thoughts and ideas have arisen from tragic circumstances; these disasters were never severe enough to extinguish positive human spirits. Inner spirits always grew larger than difficulties, intellects deeper than the disasters. Problems begging for solutions are only answered when a person's positive spirit turns attention away from what one cannot control and toward the challenges at hand.

George E. Johnson began his career in business selling black cosmetics for Fuller Products, a small company in Chicago. A few years later he transferred to the company's laboratory, where he worked as an assistant chemist with Dr. Herbert Martini. One day a barber named Orville Nelson came to the lab with a problem. Nelson wanted an improved hair straightener for blacks. Fuller Products wasn't interested in the barber's problem but George was. So he went to see Nelson at his shop. There Johnson found customers standing in line, waiting to have their hair straightened. He went to other shops with black clientele. The need was obvious, blacks wanted a hair straightener that worked. They wanted a product they could use conveniently, in their homes. Eventually, a product was formulated. The next step was to take it to market.

In early 1954, George E. Johnson sat down and estimated he would need $500 to begin marketing his product, Ultra Wave Hair Culture, a hair straightener for black men. It was more than he had, so George went to a bank to see about a loan. The loan officer wasn't impressed with George's product—maybe it was a form of prejudice—and turned him down. "You've got a good job," he told George, "You've got 10 years there. Why blow it?"

George was disappointed but he would not be deterred from pursuing his goal. He went to another bank and applied for a loan. George told this loan officer that he wanted to go to California and needed $250. The loan was granted. And with it, George, his wife, his brother, and Dr. Herbert Martini started Johnson Products, a highly successful, black owned publicly held enterprise that has provided customers with hair care products for more than 50 years.

A Positive Outlook Invites Change and Improvement

If anyone insists on finding things to worry about in his own life, the opportunities are unlimited and nothing can prevent his finding them. All too frequently people make themselves mad because things do not go their way. They try something and it doesn't work out. They give their best but their best isn't good enough. They try to help someone and that person turns against them. The possibilities for disappointment and worry extend beyond imagination. There are, equally, unlimited harmful and ineffective ways people can choose to react when failure persists. They can get mad, run away, engage an enemy in a fight—the list is long. The fundamental reason why these methods, and countless others like them, are harmful and ineffectual is that they are negative in nature. They always make things worse, and the person doing them less effective.

The value of a positive outlook is that it ignites change and improvement. It helps lift people over the rough spots by getting them to strengthen their abilities and to follow up with actions, productive actions. Consider the case of an ambitious young man who started in business selling insurance on the West Coast. His first few months were slow. Few people were interested in buying his policies. He knew, of course, that getting started would be difficult, so he stayed with it. He wasn't a quitter and he knew better than to give up too soon. He worked hard. The young man studied his product and prepared lists of prospective buyers. He worked on his selling techniques, trying to say just the right things. But try as he might, few customers bought his policies. So, he redoubled his efforts, working longer hours and calling on more prospects.

But as the months rolled by he realized he was getting nowhere—earning barely enough to meet his living expenses. Discouraged, he asked himself a question. It was a question like the ones that so many people who struggle to succeed ask themselves: What am I doing in this business? Selling insurance wasn't the work he had imagined it would be. "I want to become a wealthy man," he thought to himself. "But at the rate I'm going, I'll never get there." He wanted so much to be successful. So, he gave still more effort to selling, trying to get his prospects to buy. But the more he tried the less effective these additional efforts proved to be. He was still getting nowhere.

Then one day a very troubling question entered his head: "Could I be going about selling insurance all wrong?" The answer was obvious. It wasn't a pleasant answer, but he had to admit it was true. Then he saw himself, perhaps for the first time. "Here I am thinking only about how I can get these fine people to buy insurance from me, just so I can earn handsome commissions and be successful. Maybe I've got this selling thing backward. Maybe I ought to take a greater interest in my customers. Maybe I ought to see things from their position. Maybe I ought to put them first and not myself first." So each day, just before he made a call, he'd give a simple prayer-like reminder to himself: "What can I provide my customers with that will make their lives a little more secure, a little better?"

Taking the other person's position was unnatural at first, and it wasn't easy to do. But the more he tried, the easier it became. After a while he was hardly giving any thought to what he'd get from each sale, focusing entirely on his customers. By thinking about each sale from the customer's perspective, he started to see things differently. Then another idea came to him. He realized that the life insurance policies he sold provided an estate for ordinary people. It was the only product that could do that. People liked this idea. And, because he respected his customers and honestly cared about them, they recognized his sincerity and bought from him.

Before long his work began to change. What earlier he saw as just a job became an exciting calling. His mission in life became to see that everyone who wanted an instant estate could get one by buying life insurance. People who had been just customers a few years earlier became, in his mind and heart, his friends whom he cared about and respected. Other people must have detected this wonderful change. They wanted to buy insurance from him, too. His business grew.

When he faced his difficulties head on and went to work repairing his weaknesses, he started to become a different person. And the more he changed, the more he realized that the positive approach he was taking was benefiting himself and his customers. And he became a successful salesman because of it.

Facing Difficulties

Let's review some of the ways you can respond to adversity effectively.

1. Refuse to be defeated. Keep fighting on.
2. Let life open new doors for you as other ones slam shut.
3. Don't be timid about entering new realms, trying new ventures, experimenting with different methods.
4. Get rid of sour feelings. They will drag you down.
5. Work through setbacks; keep moving ahead positively.
6. Let your positive imagination ignite your creativity and willingness to make improvements.

CHAPTER 12

Make the Most of Your Uniqueness

Find a purpose you love and pursue it wholeheartedly

Our primary business as humans is to become fully developed persons who do meaningful things. No good life has ever yet been lived that did not accept this summons wholeheartedly. Many people today, maybe most people, try their level best to be successful. And many do reach a fair measure of what they set out to attain. Yet, even after they do achieve their aims, many remain perplexed by feelings that something in their lives is missing. Exactly what that "something" is, they don't fully know.

A large part of their unease is traceable to their purposes and the ways they pursue them. Few things are more infected with error than what success is and how best to achieve it. Great quantities of ink have flowed from the pens of many writers offering us advice on how we can get what we most want in life. The formulas for success are many. We can read about them in popular books today: how to grow rich, how to move ahead, how to achieve peace of mind, how to become more attractive, or more popular, or more intelligent, or more at ease around others. There's a formula for how to get practically anything we desire. Many of these methods work. And so, people who follow this advice do move ahead, do become more intelligent, and do prosper—but that's all that comes of it, nothing more. They achieve a measure of the success they seek but that never fulfills them. A feeling of emptiness persists.

As effective as these approaches to success are—and they do work—what most troubles people is the fact that these methods never fully produce what people want most. People seek success, because they believe that is what they most want. They believe that success involves getting those things they most desire. This is the popular mood and it is seldom questioned: If you have wealth and many fine possessions, you are successful; if you have an education, you are successful. This is what most people believe. And even those who do not fully accept it have a constant struggle on their hands, every day, reminding themselves that it isn't true. How frequently a person looks at a stately mansion or a fine yacht or a vacation home with a spectacular view and thinks, "If only this could be mine." Wanting such things is one thing. Believing that having them equals success and leads to joy is another matter entirely.

Something lies deep within human nature that is easily seduced by the notion that having things equates with success and, with it, abiding happiness. Of course humans need basics to get by and to be comfortable and safe. Life in privation and poverty is wretched. There's no disputing that. Humans do well to take care of their own needs and those around them who depend upon their care. And, too, one can find great happiness in seeing to it that others are well cared for materially. But the ultimate kind of success—the thing that people really want—is complex and involves far more than getting things.

The person who believes that securing his own personal happiness is life's richest treasure worships a very small god. "If only I had this or owned that," one thinks, "then I'll be successful and hence, happy." Another person says to himself, "If only I were smarter or more knowledgeable of a subject, then I'd be successful and happy." And so, a person gets this or that or improves his vocabulary or understanding of things thought to be important but happiness does not arrive. After the thrill and excitement wear off from getting the new boat or marrying the beautiful mate or improving one's knowledge of a subject, the person finds himself right back where he began, searching for something else to do the trick. But nothing does. The fault lies in confusing enjoyment with happiness. No matter how much we may enjoy something, we still feel a hollowness that we can't explain, a restless urge for something more.

It is undeniable that people want success, the high opinion of others, and happiness. Faced with a choice, who wouldn't choose success over mediocrity, compliments over criticisms, happiness over sadness? And, because we are largely self-sufficient creatures, it isn't surprising that people learn to grasp for what they want. While we may actually get what we want, this thing called happiness usually eludes us. The commonest reason why people never achieve the happiness they desperately want is that they reach for it directly. By trying to achieve desired states of mind, such as happiness or peace or humility, in a direct way they focus on themselves. All their concern and effort are centered inwardly. They make their failure here, by their childish self-seeking efforts. Human experience shows us that the greatest forms of unhappiness do not arise so often from external sources but from overconcern with self. This always produces an unhealthy experience. The hypochondriac worries himself sick, because he cannot keep his mind on anything other than himself. In a like way the person who focuses on making himself happy ends up making himself terribly unhappy.

When we examine the biographies of great people from history whose lives we honor most, we may be surprised to find that not one of them was interested primarily in their own happiness. They may have been extraordinarily happy or found happiness after a long struggle, but they never sought it for themselves directly, as their life's chief ambition. It didn't drive them. The happiness they did experience found them. In giving themselves to a great cause, serving something lager than self, happiness came to them.

What we are dealing with here is a paradox. Think of the person who tries to be humble. This person might act in ways that will lead others to think he is humble, but humility will always elude him because he is play acting. He's not authentic; he's a phony. Even when he thinks ill of himself, humility does not arrive, because in doing that he is still overly concerned with himself and that's the opposite of humility. He is still a phony. The only way to achieve humility is to not think of oneself at all.

As with humility, the only way to achieve happiness is to not think about it, to not pursue it directly. The healthiest way to achieve happiness is to work for achieving something worthwhile, something larger and more enduring than self. A very wise person once said that happiness is a state of going somewhere, one directionally, without regret or reservation. That's the secret of a truly happy person. Indeed, the world is an impossible place to be happy in if your chief concerns focus inwardly, not outwardly.

Find Your Calling

One of the toughest challenges we have as humans is to discover and develop our talents and then make our marks in the world where they can best be made. Many a life has limped along, underpowered and disinterested, not from lack of talent but from lack of a proper match between temperament, talents, and interests and one's work. It would be much like a train of one gauge trying to move on the tracks of a different gauge.

Once in a while a person will awaken to this problem and do something about it. Consider the following story of a man who started down one set of tracks and discovered that he was on the wrong road for himself. At 36, Rob Waldron, with a Harvard MBA and experience at Morgan Stanley, had his career mapped out, and he was on track for meeting his goal. "I just wanted to run a big company and make a ton of money doing it," he said. He grew a $2 million tutoring company owned by Kaplan into a $50 million operation in less than 5 years. But then September 11th came. He mistakenly thought his wife's sister had been killed. He worried about anthrax scares, poisoned water supplies. Money suddenly was not that important to him. "I had this terrible need to feel like I was fixing something," he said. So, he changed his once all-consuming drive for power and wealth, and turned his energies toward a new target: Jumpstart, a nonprofit group in Boston.

As interesting and appealing as this story may be to some readers, we would be greatly mistaken to conclude that everyone is obliged to take up lives of public service and philanthropy. Who's to say that everyone is suited to such enterprise? Many good lives have been lived—good, rich, productive, fulfilling lives—entirely in the realm of business, making money and lots of it. When you think about it, business is the only institution that creates wealth, and without material abundance, without something to give to others, philanthropy is impossible. Many lives are well suited to some place within the wide and varied employment opportunities found in free enterprise. From the fields of advertising and human resources to science and technology, and from finance and manufacturing to design and marketing, business needs good people with all kinds of specialties and aptitudes. In fact, free-enterprise economies offer better opportunities for people who earnestly seek to fulfill their callings than any other economic arrangement. The first part of the secret to one's happiness lies in selecting work that matches one's passions. It takes integrity to pursue the right match.

At its deepest, the emptiness that people experience in their work does not arise so much from a poor match between talent and occupation (although this clearly is the case with many people) as it does from the inability to accept who one is and the unwillingness to turn attention from getting something for oneself to being the person one really is. Career guidance counselors and employment managers today perform invaluable service to people, helping them understand their capabilities and matching these to programs of study, job opportunities, and careers. The primary source of unease that people experience in their work lives, and lack of fulfillment they find there, is the inability to accept themselves for who they are and to find joy in doing what they were meant to do.

Our desires for getting things get in the way of our finding enjoyment in our uniqueness and doing something with it that serves the needs of others or some cause larger than our own appetites. Materialism is doing its best to convince us that we ought not to respect our individual gifts, whatever these passions and talents may be. And it continuously whispers in our ear that we ought to serve our own wants first and foremost and forget about the possibilities of giving our best to something greater.

It takes a fair amount of humility and a great deal of wisdom to recognize and to accept one's uniqueness—what one can do well and likes to do—and to realize that these are gifts. While we may choose to nurture our human capabilities and develop them through training, experience, and discipline, we do well to realize that they are not things we put into ourselves. We did not give ourselves our personalities, our temperaments, our intelligence, our interests, our passions. Religion has its ways of explaining the significance of all this, but our business here will focus on accepting oneself with integrity and then working and living to find the possibilities for excitement and fulfillment that follow.

In his book, *Business as a Calling*, Michael Novak tells us that callings are experiences we feel deep within ourselves. They arise out of experiences with ourselves, as we do things, interact with others, work and play. Our inner voice reveals to us, through mysterious impulses, important things: who we are, and what we ought to do, and who we can become as human beings. There is a mystical, spiritual quality to these impulses, urging us to become more of who we are, doing better what we are meant to do. If we listen, we can find our calling. A calling has the following characteristics:

- It is unique to individuals. A calling may be a cause, an ideal, an institution, the betterment of another or others.
- It is something that one's desires and talents and abilities are called to perform. In one's calling the person welcomes, loves, and experiences the frustrations and struggles associated with the work. It is a task or career in which the required drudgery is accepted gladly and performed without complaint. We willingly pay the price required in our calling.
- It brings joy and enjoyment. In following a calling one finds renewed energy. We may face dread, but we gladly know it is our duty. Therefore, we bear and overcome the fear or dread.
- It is not easy to discover. Frequently there are false paths. Trial and error are sometimes encountered until the satisfying path is found.

Defeat Pressures that Push You in Wrong Directions

Being a university professor, I advise students on which courses to take to satisfy graduation requirements, majors they might choose to pursue that match their talents and interests, and career options. Some of the students who come for advice, I discover, are terribly unhappy. They are not interested in their classes. They hate their majors. They feel lost and out of sorts with themselves. Invariably, the source of their difficulty quickly becomes obvious—they are pursuing the wrong majors. These bright, capable, potentially enthusiastic students are struggling with courses in which they have little aptitude or interest. And what

I tell them often comes as a great surprise and a huge relief. I advise them to find something they love and "go for it!"

Not long ago one such student arrived in my office asking for advice. She was having difficulty with her business classes. Her grades were marginal and she said that she found it nearly impossible to concentrate on her assignments. When I asked her what she liked to do, she said that she most enjoyed helping small children as a social worker. As she told me this, just as a bottle of champagne bubbles out when uncorked, this young woman's expression changed from gloom to joy. Her face brightened. A warm glow of enthusiasm bubbled up from deep within her, filling the room with sunny optimism. She sparkled as she shared her experiences of the previous summer, working in a depressed Chicago neighborhood.

I learned that this student had done exactly as her parents—one was an accountant, the other an attorney—had wanted her to do—study business. They wanted their daughter to earn a business degree because they believed it was a sure path to a high-paying job, something they believed was terribly important for her success and happiness. There was just one problem with their advice. It was ill suited to their daughter's aptitude and temperament. She wasn't at all interested in business. She didn't want to spend her life, as her parents were doing, making money. She wanted to spend her life helping others. She was a born social worker. One is left to wonder what our world would be like if it were not for generous souls like hers.

Clearly there are rewards that are greater than the material and the ego-satisfying, outward signs of success. We generally talk about these as psychological rewards but they go much deeper. These rewards include a deep sense of significance and lasting joy from doing what one is best fitted to do.

The Power of an Outward Focus

Finding one's uniqueness and matching it to a calling is a first step. The next challenge to meet involves escaping the clutches of an inward focus. A few years back I had a conversation with the CEO of a multi–billion dollar corporation in the prepared foods industry. We talked about how people succeed in life and he said that he, personally, never had the desire to become rich. I found that somewhat surprising. Now he was rich by ordinary standards. There wasn't any doubt about that. Why did he do so well, I wondered? The way he explained it, the reason was simple. And, when you come to think about what he said, it made a lot of sense. This is what he did: He just worked very hard at what he believed in, giving it his best efforts. He made himself unconcerned with what he'd receive in return. He said that the harder he tried and worked at what he believed in, the more successful and richer he became.

This man's experience, I learned, is not unique. Another CEO that I visited told me that he had followed the same formula, and it had served him well, too. He said that he never set out to become the CEO of his organization. Yet, that's where he ended up. What was it that propelled him to the very top, I wondered? Largely it was because those who knew and worked with this man wanted him to be their leader. He was highly esteemed by others because whatever job he was given, he focused his thoughts on what needed doing, and not on winning recognition. And, because he was 100% sincerely interested in accomplishing the jobs assigned and didn't worry about who would get the credit, he did well. Others liked his attitude. They respected him. And, as the businesses he managed within the corporation grew, his responsibilities grew. After a time, and because the businesses he managed had grown substantially, higher-ups recognized his accomplishments. They saw the abilities he had that led to his success and they knew these strengths were needed for bigger jobs. So, they promoted him to larger, more-demanding positions. Finally his company's board of directors made him president and CEO.

The secret to this man's success was that he focused his attention and efforts outwardly. By focusing on the giving of self and directing all his efforts to larger purposes, he became the kind of person who naturally attracts followers. He also became the kind of person who is better suited to work harder than others work and tend to all the menial details, which spell the difference between mediocre performance and extraordinary accomplishment. This is the kind of person who becomes an attractive human being and, in turn, attracts many more opportunities than usually flow to ordinary people. The driving and persistent concerns of superior performers are external, not internal. The more forcefully they hurl their best efforts outward, like a boomerang, the more they gain in return.

A man named Joe Snavely wrote a book titled *Milton S. Hershey, Builder*. It is about the life and works of the man whose name is practically synonymous with chocolate in this country. One day, while Joe was in the chocolate factory, he noticed a sign above Mr. Hershey's desk with this wording: "Business Is a Matter of Human Service." This, the author wrote, was the sesame of Mr. Hershey's success.

Henry Ford himself, founder of the giant automobile enterprise that bears his name, boldly lived by the creed that any business that first thought of earning a fixed dividend was bound to fail. Either profits would come from doing a job well, he believed, or they would not come at all. Henry Ford ably captured the essence of what we are talking about here over a half-century earlier, when he remarked, "A business absolutely devoted to service will have only one worry about profits. They will be embarrassingly large."

Success from Serving

One of the most helpful guides for effective living is this: Success is achieved not by serving valuables to oneself. It's reached by serving others in valuable ways. The amazing thing about success, like happiness and the genuine fulfillment people enjoy, is that it's not something they find directly. Instead, success and happiness find them. But that's not all that comes from this outward-focused, service-oriented approach to work. This approach is also the fundamental ingredient of integrity, the surest path to honesty in the workplace and in all other realms of life. If we think about it carefully, it becomes plainly evident that dishonest actions are selfish in nature. They spring from wanting to get something for oneself so strongly that a person sometimes does things that should not be done. The beauty of a service-oriented approach is that it puts self second, thereby replacing trouble-causing motives with admirable ones. And it helps people not just perform well, but perform in ways that make them better human beings who win respect and rest easy at night.

Let me tell you about another highly successful business leader who applied this powerful idea every day. Jack Reichert once headed the Brunswick Corporation. In the way of background information on Jack, it's important to mention here something he told me that says much about his approach to life. When we spoke several years ago, Jack told me, "I'm a tither to my church and have been for about 25 years. And the more I give, the more comes back to me. I don't give because I get. But, the more I give, it seems the more I get. The more I'm willing to serve, the luckier I become. My management philosophy is this: One leads by serving." People who turn from living primarily for self to serving something worthwhile make not a little change but a radical and a big change. Their interests and abilities broaden. They become deeper human beings, able to do more because of expanded abilities and heightened motivations.

Here is a little known, yet powerfully revealing, dimension of another well-known business personality, John D. Rockefeller, the very Gibraltar of capitalism. While in his late teens, in Cleveland, Rockefeller worked in a commercial house and attended Folsom's Commercial College. Each month, from his weekly earnings of $3.50, he contributed $1.80 for religious purposes, which included his Baptist Sunday school and the Five Points Mission in the New York slums. Through summers and winters young Rockefeller wore the same, shabby coat, yet his contributions continued.

Success is a paradox. The harder one tries to grab success for self, the more it escapes him. Yet, by forgetting the self and concentrating on serving a great calling with all one's energies, success seems to follow. United Parcel Service Company founder, Jim Casey, once asked his employees, "Are we working for money alone? If so, there is no surer way not to get it." Profit, like happiness, is the byproduct of purposeful living. To get it, forget it. Others have seen this idea too, and they are using it effectively.

Several years ago I received a letter from Fred Smith, the man who transformed the ideas he wrote about in a term paper for an economics course at Yale University into a reality. His professor gave him a "C" on his paper, but Fred turned his idea into a multi–billion dollar enterprise. Fred sent me materials that explained the idea behind how Federal Express gets the best efforts from its employees. The idea of service is at the center of their company philosophy and day-to-day practices.

At Federal Express the succinct and comprehensive people-service-profit (P-S-P) concept governs every activity. Each Federal Express manager is expected to follow scrupulously this formula: Take care of our people. They, in turn, will deliver the impeccable service demanded by our customers, who will reward us with the profitability necessary to secure our future. People-Service-Profit—these three words are the very foundation of Federal Express. The order is important. The first leads to the second, and both of these lead to the third.

Everywhere one looks, the relationship between an outward-looking service-oriented focus and success is strikingly clear. Speaking before Dr. Robert Schuller's Hour of Power audience at the Crystal Cathedral recently, Bert Boeckmann, owner of Galpin Motors, Inc., the world's largest Ford dealership, emphasized the importance service played in making his organization successful. Mr. Boeckmann said, " ... the one thing I tried to do was to serve the customer the way I'd want to be served, and to me that's the only reason we had to be in the business. If you're doing it for any other reason the tendency is to fail. If you're looking for a paycheck or a profit and that's where your focus is, it's in the wrong place ..." (www.hourofpower.org).

Transform Ordinary Work into a Grand Adventure

There is a basic fact about how human beings are inspired to give their finest efforts. Here's the secret: People perform best when they are totally committed to some great cause that's larger than themselves, something they believe in so much that no sacrifice is too great. J. C. Penney was thinking along these lines when he wrote, "To gain success one must serve." "Adventure" comes by putting money second and the success of a great endeavor first—not the other way around.

There are examples aplenty that demonstrate the fact that employees give their finest effort when they connect what they do with a great purpose. This happens because it transforms work into a grand adventure. William B. Walton, Sr., co-founder of Holiday Inns, understood the powerful motivational force that lies latent in each human. And he knew how to unleash it. The answer was by getting them to serve. And he said so, "We saw ourselves—all of us, from the chairman of the board to cleaning people—as a company of people. We were in a crusade to bring to the American traveling public a highway haven, a home away from home to rest and refresh them."

Business leaders frequently conceive of a mission beyond profit through the goods and services they produce, inspiring themselves and their employees to unbelievable heights. When Steven Jobs, of Apple Computer fame, put the project team together that first created the Macintosh computer, the vision was nothing less than the user-friendly transformation of personal computing so that computer technology would be accessible to everyone. When Robert Mercer headed Goodyear, he said at one point: "Here's a company that's providing freedom and mobility to people in this country and around the world." Avon has a guiding motto that captures the underlying values of all they do. It is: "Avon is a caring company that helps people around the world to feel better about themselves." And at Deluxe Check Printers, the commitment is, "To serve our customers as the best supplier of financial documents and related products and services."

But such commitments are not simply the province of the captains of industry. They often belong to normal, everyday workers as well. A woman who applies nonreflective coatings to eyeglass lenses demonstrated such commitment when she explained the importance of her role in running the coating machine by saying: "It is people's eyes we're talking about. If I don't do my job right, people might not be able to see very well!" I can just imagine this woman visualizing the people who later put on and see through those glasses she has coated. As she works, she thinks about how they see better with protected lenses because of what she's doing. And thinking these thoughts, she feels her work is significant, as she ought.

Pursue Your Passion

Let's think about how you can start—right now—applying the ideas in this chapter. How can you become a service-oriented person? What has to happen? I see three basic steps. The first step is to find your talents and interests, respond to a calling. It will be doing something that just feels right to you. Your heart will tell you so.

Second put this calling ahead of yourself. By an act of discipline, you have to not look at the world in terms of, what's in this for me? Instead, ask how you can be of value to everyone with whom you come in contact. It helps if you connect what you do with a great purpose. Make whatever you do into a great adventure for yourself and others with whom you work. Think of your work as a great cause. Go ahead. Define what you do in noble language. You are no hypocrite if you are only half-serious at first. Try living for the great purposes you set for yourself as best you can. After a while you'll get better at it. Soon, you'll actually be living, without being concerned about yourself and all that you can grab. And when you do this, I guarantee something will happen to you that has never fully happened to you before in your life. You are going to be happy, really happy! And you'll start to be successful.

The third step in learning how to serve might sound odd but trust me, it works. Just go out and do it. Go out and start serving. It doesn't have to be anything big. Any kind of service will move you forward. You learn how to serve in only one way: through doing, not from listening. And remember, don't expect anything in return. If it comes your way, then fine. If not, say to yourself, "That's okay, too. The privilege of being able to serve is reward enough," and believe it!

CHAPTER 13

Earn Trust

Build a reputation for being believable and dependable

Many years ago a self-made industrialist ran a thriving business. He told his employees that he valued their loyalty and they believed him. He told them that the company he owned was successful because they gave their best efforts and they worked even harder than before. He paid his people well and treated them well. But when bad times struck and sales plummeted and the business owner faced creditors, he knew drastic measures were necessary. He thought about letting people go but that would break the trust he had worked so hard to develop. Instead, he held true to the words he had spoken to his people earlier. He went without paying himself for several months and he cut every other possible expenditure so he could keep everyone who worked for him on his payroll. He believed that he should act as he spoke and that better times for his business would return. They did.

A reputation for being trustworthy is one of the most priceless assets you can have. With it, you can enjoy the full confidence of others. Whenever you give your word, people will believe you. Your promises will count for something and everyone will want to do business with you. Without a good reputation, you'll be plagued by a heavy cloud of suspicion. Your dependability will always be in doubt. And, of course, with those doubts in mind, most everyone will prefer not to deal with you. They'll seek out others in whom their confidence is warranted.

Trust. It's an invaluable quality, vital to one's success in any pursuit. Trust is hard to nail down exactly; it is an intangible concept but, yet, it is quite real. So, what is trust? Where does it come from? How does one get it? What's the key?

Maybe the following illustration will help us understand something more about this vital quality—trust.

Let's imagine that you've made a promise to be somewhere on a particular date. You've agreed to it well in advance and it's marked on your calendar. But before that date arrives, something else comes up—it's something else that you'd really prefer to do. This poses a conflict. You cannot be in two places at the same time. So, you have to choose. I think we all face this kind of situation at one time or another.

Several years ago I read about a woman named Gertrude Boyle who faced one of these situations and here's how she handled it. Gertrude was the chairman of Columbia Sportswear Company, the largest outerwear company in the United States, at the time. They make ski clothing and sportswear, hunting jackets, fishing vests, and footgear. Since taking the helm of Columbia Sportswear in 1970, her company had grown from $600 thousand in revenues to more than $250 million, growing at a rate of 30% to 40% annually. These were extraordinary accomplishments, and so, it was little wonder that the president invited her to the White House for a dinner honoring outstanding entrepreneurs. There was just one complication: Gertrude had already made a commitment to the American Diabetes Association.

I can just imagine what would likely go on in many minds. Those wanting very much to accept the president's invitation would likely say to themselves: "Let's see; what kind of a respectable excuse might I make up to get out of what I have promised to do? After all, it isn't every day one is invited to the White House to receive a prestigious honor." And so, it would have been easy for Gertrude Boyle to tell the association, "Sorry, something better has come up. I'll do something for you next year." But that was not her style. Instead, she told the president's staff that she had already given her word to the American Diabetes Association. She would be unable to accept the president's invitation.

If you want to cause other people to shun you, if you want them to not want to do business with you, if you want them to tell others not to trust you, here is the recipe: stick to your promises only when it's convenient to do so. If something better comes along or if you will be inconvenienced by doing what you promised or if you find that you will benefit more by doing something other than what you agreed to, then do what pleases you. That's the recipe!

We Are Known by What We Do

Do you recall a time when someone let you down, when someone agreed to do something and then failed to follow through as promised, or when someone reneged on a commitment? What did this person do about it? Was a nice-sounding excuse offered up to explain away the failure? Did the person go so far as to try to push the blame for their failure onto you or someone else? This brings to light something we have to realize. Everyone sees us by what we do. Others are little convinced by what we say. Our excuses really won't get us very far, because words mean very little compared with actions.

There is a basic psychological principle at work that explains why people develop trust in someone or some organization. Positive opinions must be confirmed by first-hand observation or by the observations from reliable friends. Without confirming observations, these opinions are lightly held and easily changed. The important thing to keep in mind is that positive opinions are earned and they need to be re-earned regularly.

Let me illustrate by way of a personal example. Many years ago I enjoyed the hospitality of a lovely couple, named Jim and Margot Gratton, in New Zealand. Jim is a superb fly fisherman and he took me to several of his favorite fishing spots. We camped and fished and enjoyed 3 days of the beautiful New Zealand spring weather. I noticed that their tent was old and didn't have a bottom to it. So, when I returned home I ordered a good quality, two-person tent from L. L. Bean and had it shipped to Jim and Margot so they could start using it right away, that summer. They love to camp and I knew that they'd get a lot of good out of it.

When I received confirmation of my order from L. L. Bean a few days later, I noticed that the tent had been shipped surface mail by mistake, instead of by air. That meant the tent would not arrive there for 3 or 4 months. Dissatisfied, I telephoned L. L. Bean right away and spoke to a courteous representative. She assured me that the problem would be corrected immediately—and it was. L. L. Bean shipped another tent, air freight, right away at Bean's expense and the gift arrived within days. My friends were delighted. Now, just think of how much more of my trust L. L. Bean earned by the way they handled the problem.

It is true, people know us by what we do. The important thing to remember here is that everyone knows us by how we live, by whether we live up to our commitments. There is no way of keeping this hidden. And it's impossible to lie or excuse your way out of a shortcoming—unless, of course, you are dealing with someone who wants to be fooled into thinking only the best about you.

Every normal person appears to have similar aspirations when it comes to relationships: to be regarded favorably by others, to be enriched and inspired by others, to be free of strife and pain from others, and to benefit from companionship and the camaraderie of others. These and the many other benefits that positive, effective relationships bring do not come cheaply or easily. They must be earned. And the price is usually high—the exact currency demanded difficult to discern. While we do know something about how best to live with others, it is remarkable that doing so frequently transcends our ability. Yet all persons of depth and insight willingly strive for the knowledge and the will to pay that price. A person who struggles every day to build effective and satisfying relationships is one to be admired.

Trust and Performance

It is a widely accepted truth that superior organizational performance arises from exceptional commitments by employees. How can management get this level of commitment? The popular prescriptions now include things like employee involvement and empowerment. The idea is for management to include all employees as part of the team. Instead of an "us" versus "them" orientation—a management versus labor atmosphere—the idea is to create a "we" organization, where everyone from the bottom to the top is part of the same team. Everyone works for the good of the organization.

Unfortunately, this ideal is not always achieved. I think part of the reason for this lies in the failure of a person to be authentic. Let me explain by relating a recent experience. Just this week I saw something that one of our students had taped to the wall of the building in which I work. It was a two-frame cartoon. The first picture showed a manager shaking hands with an employee and saying, "You are part of the team now. We are going to involve you in what goes on here. You are empowered to act freely." The next picture had the same manager telling the employee, "We have to downsize now. We don't need you anymore. You're fired."

I think this student saw the hypocrisy that grips many business people, just as it grips virtually everyone else in scores of other ways. We humans seem to have a tendency to act in particular ways because of what we expect to get. If it's believed that more can be gotten by being friendly, for instance, then we'll be friendly. It's all very calculating. We do whatever is needed, within reason, to get what we want.

Let's examine what this approach involves. One does not act out of any moral conviction but out of what is anticipated to provide the greatest benefit to self. As I have repeatedly shown earlier, integrity involves an entirely different approach. That approach involves treating others in ways that are thought to be right for their own sake, not because of the immediate returns expected. Again, it is this "me," "me," "me" business that gets humans into so much trouble.

Long ago Abraham Lincoln is reported to have said something like, "You can fool some of the people all of the time and all of the people some of the time, but you cannot fool all of the people all of the time." The point is that people see through phony schemes. They, just like the student who taped the cartoon to a wall, can spot hypocrites—and they don't trust them. Hypocrisy and integrity are poles apart. Effective relationships are built on authenticity, on trust.

Our Choices Show What We Honor Most

It's easy to see what people are most concerned with by their choices, by what they choose to do. That's fairly well understood and it leads us to another important principle about trust. It is this: We reserve our highest opinions for those who are faithful to their commitments, for those who follow through with promises made. Naturally, we feel we can rely on them because of it. Making promises comes easily; measuring up to promises is far more revealing of what a person is all about. Yet, this happens in many small ways with each of us daily. Each of us is continually writing a story of our trustworthiness in the minds of others by how we choose to follow through with our commitments.

One of the most inspiring illustrations of the power of being faithful to an agreement comes out of the history of the Timken Roller Bearing Company in Canton, Ohio. We must go back in time, many decades ago, to understand this situation. The Timken Roller Bearing Company had entered into a contract to supply Ford Motor Company with axles. Timken was a small struggling company. Its modest product line consisted mostly of roller bearings, but Timken was beginning to branch out into a new line, axles. Timken hadn't yet manufactured them on a large-scale, mass-production basis. That was about to change with the recently signed Ford contract—an important first step in Timken's future expansion. It planned to grow by supplying major manufacturers with reliable high-quality parts. Timken's owners knew that success depended on quality and reliability, particularly when it came to delivery promises and standing behind their products.

Because it had the lowest bid, Timken won the Ford contract. A few months passed after the contracts were signed and production was under way. Soon thereafter, Timken shipped the first batch of axles to Ford. It looked as though a satisfying and profitable deal was going well. But a disturbing piece of news broke the happy chain of events. Timken's accountants discovered that the actual costs of production were running much higher than anticipated. Unforeseen expenses showed up. All tolled, Timken's accountants figured that their company had underbid the Ford contract by 40%. Inexperienced at the time, Timken terribly underestimated what its costs would be.

Timken Roller Bearing faced a problem: What to do? It could go back to Ford and say, "We underbid by mistake. We want to be paid 40% more, now that we have your business." Or, Timken could just figure a deal is a deal, and do the only honorable thing—take it out of their own pockets.

There comes a time when you just have to grit your teeth and follow through with a bargain. And that's exactly what Timken's leaders decided they would do. Despite the fact it was just a small firm, struggling with cash flow problems of its own, Timken's management held to their end of the bargain. They made the best of a bad situation even though it cost them dearly in the short run.

When you think about it, a substantial price increase would have upset Ford's budget. That would not have been fair. It would not have been fair to Timken's competitors either, who bid somewhat higher for Ford's business. And, too, there were long-range considerations to be concerned about—like being known as a company that would stick by its agreements. Making good on this commitment to Ford would be a feather in Timken's cap, one that would help them win future contracts with Ford and other large-scale manufacturers.

So, that's how Timken chose to deal with the problem. Ford later learned about it, and that caused them to realize they were dealing with an honorable firm. Word spread. More business came to Timken from Ford. Other manufacturers wanted to do business with Timken, too. Timken became known as a company that could be counted on to live by its agreements.

As the foregoing story teaches us, faithfulness is an important dimension in all human interactions, especially in business. And it's one's consistency in adhering to promises made that leads others to want to continue dealing with that person or organization.

Promises and Performance

The mechanic who promises to have your car ready at 5:00 o'clock on Thursday afternoon but doesn't; the gardener who says he'll be at your house on Saturday morning to trim your hedge but fails to show; the tax accountant who promises to remember to include a stock transaction in your tax return but forgets—what are we to think of them? If you want the confidence of others, then you'll have to earn it by performing as promised.

Many of the problems that we have with others these days tend to arise from an attitude of "I'm not to blame. Something went wrong beyond my control or someone else caused me to do it. I'm a victim. It's not my fault." Yes, there are plenty of slip-ups. There are situations where things don't go as we had planned or hoped they might go. Regardless of whether a slip up is unintentional, it still takes a long time to overcome its negative effects. It may require dozens of good experiences afterward to mend the trust lost because of one unpleasant experience that harmed a fine reputation in the first place. A product is not shipped when promised, a part is left out of an order—these amount to broken promises, actual or implied, and they can damage one's reputation instantly. Worse yet, this kind of damage can linger on for many years—especially if excuses are made instead of positive, corrective actions taken.

Here's another valuable principle about achieving success to hold in your thoughts: Successful people do not make excuses after making mistakes. Instead they take responsibility for what went wrong and they genuinely feel bad about the unfortunate circumstances they caused. The reason for the connection between success and owning up to shortcomings can be traced directly to the process of improvement, something that leads to superior performance and, hence, success. The person who admits to errors sets into motion the beginning steps of self-improvement. Those who do not do this are unable and unwilling to improve themselves. And, because of that, they become permanently stuck in the web of mediocrity.

Now, contrast the unwillingness of a mediocre performer to own up to failures and, hence, improve to the stand-up-and-accept-responsibility approach of a world-class competitor. Liz Claiborne, Inc. serves as a superb example. Not long ago a reporter from the *Wall Street Journal* wanted to learn how businesses handle letters of complaint. One was mailed to clothing manufacturer, Liz Claiborne. The letter read, in part, "I like your dress but the buttonholes keep unraveling."

Within days, a reply from Claiborne arrived: "We're sorry to have disappointed you even once, and we will strive in the future to deserve your trust." Even though the complaint letter mentioned that the dress was well worn, Claiborne's response gushed on apologetically: "Loose buttons or imperfect buttonholes are unacceptable." The company told the writer of the letter to go have the buttonholes mended by a good tailor and promised full reimbursement.

All Promises Should Matter

At Miami University in Oxford, Ohio, where I teach, we have something called an Executive-in-Residence Program. It involves having a top-level business leader visit our campus for 2 days during a semester. The visiting executive attends selected classes in the business school, gives lectures, and meets with students and faculty to discuss current issues. Naturally, our students are keenly interested to hear "how it really is" in the business world from these captains of industry. They are, indeed, impressive individuals.

I recall one such visit when students asked Dick Heckert, who was chairman and CEO of DuPont at the time, about how to succeed. "What advice do you have for us who are about to enter business?" one student asked. Our visiting executive didn't hesitate a moment before answering.

"My advice is fairly simple," he said. "Do what you say you are going to do. Keep your promises, especially if it's inconvenient for you. Go out of your way to act responsibly. If you do that, if you make good on every obligation, others will see that. They will come to realize you are dependable. People will know you can be trusted to keep your word."

And with that simple advice, Heckert launched into something deeper. He had more to tell the young men and women there, something he thought was very important. And everyone in the room listened intently. "We have a way of identifying people where I work," he said. "We call it the 'flower theory.' If you look at a flower from above, it appears beautiful. But, if you look at it from below, it isn't so pretty. When we look at managers we always wonder, 'How do those looking up, from below, see them?' A boss looks at a subordinate and that subordinate appears to be doing a good job. And that's good. But how do the subordinates, looking from below, see that manager?" Well, we had a lot to think about from what he said that day.

I can tell you here what it got me to think about. I saw, right then and there, that each of us has a tendency to be especially careful in meeting our obligations to those on whom we depend. We tend to be a little more casual about our obligations to those who depend on us. We know where rewards come from, don't we? So, the flower theory has merit, revealing what we are really like by how we treat those who are not in a position to reward us.

Think about this idea. By holding to every commitment—especially commitments made to those whom one does not particularly need for something—one establishes a powerful habit of obedience to obligations. What power such an unbending habit of holding fast to all promises made can have in earning trust. And the stronger that habit is, the less inclined a person becomes to break agreements when the force of temptation is especially strong.

Be a Responsible Neighbor

An important fundamental of good citizenship can be gleaned from the story of J. C. Penney, as a boy, raising pigs in Hamilton, Missouri. From the start, Penney's pig business was very successful. He could turn a dollar and a half into twenty dollars' profit. But his father eventually came to him and said, "You cannot continue with it because it's offensive to our neighbors."

Every business is someone's neighbor, just as is every individual in a work setting. What kind of a neighbor is your business? What kind of neighbor are you? Would you want to have yourself for a neighbor? The answer you get to that question is a fair measure of what kind of neighbor you are. Most of us would prefer neighbors who aren't nuisances. This is why concerned businesses regard goodwill and positive relationships with their neighbors as important obligations of citizenship. Now for the real test: what happens when a business learns that it is not being such a good neighbor? Does it change? Or, does it go its own way, pleasing itself first?

Here's how one company answered that question. In Akron, Goodyear's chairman and CEO, Robert Mercer, learned of a tank containing methylisocyanate at a company plant. This is the same chemical that caused the deaths of thousands in Bhopal, India. Mercer's reaction was swift and firm. "Get rid of it!"

"But," came the response from the plant, "we need it to make the accelerator for one of our most profitable products."

Mercer stood firm, "It's gone. Shut it down. Bail that stuff out of there and get rid of it."

"But," plant personnel persisted, "if that happens, we'll have to close the plant."

Mercer would not retreat. "Close it! There's no appeal to it. We're not going to have that stuff in the middle of a residential area."

The power of public outcries tends to prevent companies from being bad neighbors. I think that if the public learned of the dangerous chemical in Akron, many members of the community would be alarmed, and rightly so. Robert Mercer knew this, of course. But his example illustrates someone who did what was believed to be the "right thing"—the neighborly thing—to do without having to be forced to comply. As a consequence, he avoided the threat of a public outcry.

Too often, however, humans feel they can hide things such as this and so they become inclined to carry on with practices that would receive strong opposition. By being a good neighbor in the first place, a business gets on with doing what's right without having all the hassle and bad publicity that plague less sensitive organizations.

Here's another true story that illustrates this powerful idea of acting in ways toward others that naturally elicits their trust. Many years ago, when he was a young man working for Johnson & Higgins of California in Los Angeles, Dick Ross had an outstanding year. Around Christmastime he was informed by top management that he would receive a nice bonus for his very productive year.

Now most young men would have immediately begun to visualize how such a windfall might be used, especially with a young family at Christmastime. But Dick Ross didn't do that. Instead he told top management that he didn't feel he could accept the entire bonus himself because, although he had some success, it was largely due to the team of people that had given him the backup to be able to get the job done. The only way he would accept the bonus would be on the basis that it would be shared with the group. And that's what was done. The bonus was shared. Now, what do you suppose those people working for this young man thought about him?

As the years rolled by, this man's unselfishness rubbed off into other areas of his life. He was active in community affairs. He was a leader in his social circles. Everybody who knew him saw what a fine man Dick was and everyone wanted to be his friend. Customers wanted to buy from him. His superiors recognized his outstanding performance. They saw how much business he was bringing into the firm. In time he was promoted. The pattern continued. It was an unbroken story of service and success and his promotions continued, right along with his firm's sales and earnings growth. He rose in his organization, all the way to the very top, retiring as his company's chairman of the board.

Build a Reputation for Believability

How can you gain the trust and confidence of others? Let's review the formula.

1. Honor all your promises, be they expressly stated or just implied. Remember that trust needs to be earned and re-earned. It grows when others confirm a positive opinion of someone by that person's actions. Excuses get one nowhere; only follow through counts.

2. Place holding to commitments above convenience, cost to self, and your preference to do something else.

3. Never make excuses for your failures or shortcomings. Learn from your failures and let the experience work amendment in you for self-improvement. Remember that there is a connection between on-going improvement and superb performance and, hence, success.

4. Form the right kinds of habits. Unbending dedication to promises brings consistent follow through with obligations.

5. Be particularly careful to honor your promises and implied obligations to others who depend on you. It is easy to be concerned with relationships in which you stand to gain something and lax about relationships with those in whom you stand to gain little or nothing. Be careful. Selfishness can gain a foothold and drive a wedge between you and your adherence to promises.

6. Live above the ordinary. Keep your promises, stated and implied, with the faceless masses, with the public in general.

7. Be a good neighbor, a good citizen, and a protector of the world's resources for future generations. These are the commitments we all need to honor as members of society and inhabitants of the planet Earth.

CHAPTER 14

Defeat What Destroys

Put your pride in its place

A few years ago a man wrote me a letter that revealed a good deal of bitterness. In particular, he was bothered by an article that I had written about some of the fine and decent things being done in corporate America by successful business leaders. He wanted to tell me about some of the negative things that he had seen going on in business during his career. He said that there are some bad apples in the executive ranks, and he wanted to tell me about one in particular. To add credibility to his story, the man told of his experience, which had spanned over 40 years in retailing and international trade. He said that he had recently retired as the president of a multi–million dollar division of a multi–billion dollar corporation that was then going through Chapter 11. He had reported to the corporate CEO.

This man said that at the very beginning his CEO did not forget his humble start in life. And, the CEO displayed great empathy for all levels. But over time the years changed him, and he began to believe his own publicity. It got to the point where his boss was enjoying perks at the expense of the rank and file, those who were directly responsible for producing sales. At the very end, the CEO "cashed out" the company at a favorable price. Now it was clear that the CEO this man had in mind became greedy and let success go to his head.

Others, too, have observed this same phenomenon—success going to a person's head. A senior writer at *Business Week* named John Byrne, for example, wrote an article, "The CEO Disease." It was about how egotism can breed corporate disaster. John's story, about out-of-control egos, struck a reverberating cord with his magazine's readers. It stirred many letters to the editor from people telling about their experiences, and this is what some of them said:

> In too many organizations, a corporate nobility has evolved that sees itself as omniscient and cuts more off the corporate-compensation loaf for itself, despite the talk about teamwork, participatory management, and the dispersion of decision-making responsibility.

> In the era of personality journalism, the media have helped feed the affliction of success; goaded by public-relations people, who must deal with the consequences, the media have publicized larger-than-life stories about our company's head that he believes, now, are true.

> It's too bad that in today's world of large corporations and large labor unions, the sole objective of many in power is to stay in power and take all they can get. This objective is often carried out with little or no concern for the average company employee or the rank-and-file union member.

> The head of our company seems to be going through what's known as "burnout"—the feeling of "is that all there is to life?" His inability to find meaning has led him to grab for more power and exhibit delusions of grandeur. Deep down, he seems depressed.

These comments about top-level leaders indicate an affliction—call it "the disease of success." This disease is a common human failing. It's what pride can do to anyone and it leads to out-of-control egos. Most of life's troubles are caused not by external forces but by internal ones, arising out of our selves. Pride can transform ordinarily nice people into painful fatheads and insufferable snobs, whom no one can stand to be around or work alongside.

Pride: What Is it?

A little girl at a child's birthday party was unable to finish her piece of cake. One of the mothers there asked her, "Why did you take such a big piece of cake? Didn't you know you are too little to eat all of it?"

The little girl thought for a moment and replied, "That's because I'm bigger on the outside than I am on the inside." This is what pride is like. It's pretending to be bigger on the outside than we are on the inside.

Pride—it's a terrible thing. It's also a very sneaky thing that comes upon us when we appear to be our strongest. Pride creeps into people's hearts and minds and begins its insidious work right after they reach success, because it is at these times they are most vulnerable. Here is how this works. We accomplish something. We win a great battle. We reach what we set out to achieve. And now, for a moment, we feel good about it, maybe too good. But soon the enjoyment starts to wear off. We realize it is slipping away and we don't want to lose that feeling. To keep it alive, we admire what we, ourselves, have done. We keep complimenting ourselves and it still feels good. Quickly, this leads us to conclude that we are a good bit smarter and a lot better than we actually are. But all the while, something terrible is at work inside our heart and mind, reminding us of how wonderful we are and we start to believe it. But at the same time there is also something else inside us that wants to cast doubts about our over estimates of ourselves. To eliminate this voice, we tell others how great we are, hoping to convince them. If we can get them to believe we are wonderful, then it must be true. How foolish we make ourselves when we insist on seeking praise for what we have done instead of looking ahead, our eyes on a stiffer challenge.

We all have a tendency to allow pride to spoil our accomplishments. I learned this important—and painful—lesson soon after I got out of graduate school. My first job after earning a Ph.D. in Business from the University of Illinois was with the Anaconda Copper Company in New York City, where my chief responsibility was supervisory training. We developed and held foreman training courses in Anaconda's mining operations throughout the west. I decided to write a newsletter for all those who had completed the training. It would be a good vehicle to communicate important information to Anaconda's supervisory force and to encourage them to apply what they had learned. My idea received immediate support from higher-ups and I prepared the first issue. Being filled with pride and a sense of importance, I made the mistake of signing my name on the last page of the newsletter, "Dr. Charlie Watson."

Feeling good about the first issue of the newsletter, I sent a copy of it to my former professor and friend, Earl Planty. He didn't view the newsletter the way I had hoped he would. Earl saw something about me that he didn't like and he was quick to point it out. He ripped off the last page of the newsletter and circled the very conspicuous "Dr." in front of my name and dashed off a stinging hand written note to me about my error in judgment. What Earl said to me was tough and direct and true. It read:

This cries out, it shouts: Look at me and my title! I am somebody—a scholar, an academic. Don't you dirty semi-literate miners just love us book readers. I know you do. So love me! I don't work with my hands the way you do, just my head! Ain't it beautiful. Always remember that Dr. before the name, fellows, if you are ever thinking of being personal and openly communicative with me— none of that fraternal, "Charlie" stuff with me. I'm Dr. Watson. You all keep your distance. Remember now, Dr., not Charlie. How am I ever going to get your respect if you forget the title? So I wrote it clear and big and at an important spot at the end so you wouldn't forget. I have a title—not you, of course.

I can still recall that heated flush that overcame me when I read Earl's note and realized it was true. I had made a huge mistake. Pride had gotten the better of me. To elicit admiration from others, I tried to deceive them into thinking I was better that I actually was. And I didn't fool anyone. I only made a fool of myself.

Conquering Out-of-Control Egos

Look around, and you will see many people who'd like you to think that they are a good bit more important, a lot wealthier, and far smarter than they actually are. They probably are a bit unsure themselves that they are these things but if they can get you to think they are, that's good enough. This is what pride, swollen out of control, can do to people. It is plainly evident that most of us do have a tendency to want others to think well of us. We seek their approval, their respect, and their admiration. Even when our pride projects itself in less dramatic ways, it is still there doing its work and usually producing quite the opposite effect than what we want. History is filled with examples showing that a great many of life's tumbles are caused by people getting tripped up over their own egos.

Pride comes in all forms. There is a pride that comes from one's birth and ancestry, another from position and money, another from beauty and charm, another from accomplishment, another from physical prowess and skill, another from knowledge and intellect. There are many more forms of pride too. As bad as pride itself may be, the contempt for others—others who are less gifted and accomplished—that pride breeds is far worse. It seems to be a universal pattern that each person holds up a standard by which he gauges all others and that standard always involves measures by which the evaluator believes himself to be most gifted.

There is a solution to the problem pride presents us with and the contempt it breeds toward others. The first step is to realize that the powers and talents that made possible our accomplishments did not arise from our own doing. They are gifts. We are not the ultimate source of these gifts. While we might develop our gifts—our talents and passions and inherent abilities—and use them wisely, we are not their source. Who can honestly say that he gave himself his special talents? Who can honestly claim that she devised her heart to love those things she regards most highly and that arouse her most intense passions? Did George Gershwin or Loretta Lynn or Elton John give themselves their abilities to write music? Did Yogi Berra put his love for baseball into his heart? Did Steve Jobs put into himself his inspiration for and capacity to create Apple Computers and, then 25 years later, the iPod? While it is true that these people worked hard at what they did and their efforts were in no small way responsible for furthering their abilities and eventual accomplishments, it is also true that they did not give themselves their talents and their capacity to find joy in what they did. Something greater than themselves did that, something worth respecting. For to not respect it openly invites the most destructive form of pride. This is the belief that nothing is greater, or smarter, or more powerful, or more deserving of reverence than our selves.

I once discussed the idea of out-of-control egos with Mike Wright, who was chairman and CEO of Super Valu Foods in Minneapolis at the time. He said, "All of us in life, whether you're a teacher, or a businessman, or a priest, or anything else, should worry about whether our egos have gotten out of control. I think more problems result from an imbalance of the ego than a lot of other things. It can destroy companies and families and individuals."

Jack Sparks, who ran Whirlpool, once mentioned to me, "Always be yourself. Don't try to be something you're not, because people are going to spot you if you start to pretend to be something you're not." Smart people know this principle. They know how to control their egos, something that is extremely difficult to control as one moves ahead. Jim Casey, the man who founded the United Parcel Service, advised: "Don't overrate yourself. Lean a little the other way. Be constructively dissatisfied and you'll go further." Another thing honest people do to control their egos is to acknowledge that their continued success will always require the help of others. As Jim Casey once told his employees, "You cannot be successful entirely through your own efforts. All of us, if we are to accomplish anything worthwhile, will do it largely through the help and cooperation of other people who work with us."

An industrialist went to Gettysburg, PA, in 1968 to see Dwight D. Eisenhower. Author James Hames was on hand. During a discussion on war the visitor stated, "Herodotus said in the Peloponnesian Wars that 'you can't be an armchair general 20 miles from the front.'"

Later, Hames asked Eisenhower about the quotation.

"First, it wasn't Herodotus, but Aemilius Paulus," said the retired five-star general. "Second, it wasn't the Peloponnesian but the Punic Wars. And third, he misquoted."

Surprise registered on Hames' face. Eisenhower continued, "You must understand, I got where I did by hiding my ego." The former president saw no reason to flaunt his knowledge or embarrass his guest.

It is true. Practically everyone wants to be somebody special, to feel important, and to enjoy prestige. Practically everyone wants to have nice things, the money to buy whatever he wants. And, practically everyone wants recognition, to be looked up to with admiration. Pride tricks us into thinking that feeling important, is important. Pride deceives us into believing that material possessions and recognition really are all there is. What's worse, it leads us into thinking that the more we get the more satisfied we'll become with ourselves. And so, many folks try these things but none work.

So, what can you do if you have an ego that's out of control? Just recognizing it—even faintly suspecting the possibility—I'd say, is a positive step. Another thing to consider is the cost of an out of control ego. Just think of what egotism does to a person, how it causes that person to behave—and we have all witnessed this kind of behavior. It can be a terrible blight on anyone. One excellent way of overcoming the tendency to act more important than you really are is to think about arrogant, egotistical people you have known and to ask your self, "Do I want to allow that to happen to me?"

Mike Wright, of Super Valu Stores, suggested a simple question any of us can ask ourselves to stop pride from infecting our hearts and minds in the first place. The question is: What am I doing to be a jerk around here? Not a bad question! Mike went on to tell me, "I found it works surprisingly well and the more I ask it the better I seem to get at answering it honestly."

John Bunyan, the man who over 300 years ago wrote *Pilgrim's Progress*, greeted his parishioners after preaching a Sunday sermon. A man in the congregation complimented him, saying that he had just delivered a great sermon. Bunyan replied, "I know. The Devil already told me that as I was walking down the steps."

Admit Your Limitations

It is astounding what a leader can accomplish if his ego doesn't get in the way. Despite his calling the Soviet Union an "evil empire," President Ronald Reagan was deeply committed to improving relations with Moscow. But what did he know of this vast superpower? Privately, he realized that he knew little, but he was also wise enough to know the stakes were high. His National Security Adviser, Robert McFarland, also understood that his boss, the president, barely knew fact one about the Soviet Union. What to do? The National Security Council's Soviet expert, Jack F. Matlock, Jr. had administration experts create a series of reports dubbed "Soviet Union 101." Now, President Reagan had his homework to do. And, like a conscientious schoolboy, he read and digested all 21 reports, making notes and asking the authors lots of questions. The president met with other specialists on Soviet culture and learned from them, too. Then, on the eve of his first summit with Gorbachev in 1985, Reagan held a mock summit, with Matlock playing Gorbachev. It worked: Reagan was better prepared than Gorbachev.

The surest way for anyone to rise above those forces that prevent improvement is to humble himself before useful suggestions. Otherwise, one can be certain of not only retaining his shortcoming but also being further dominated by pride, which makes improvement impossible. There are practical things that anyone with courage can do. The first one is to admit you might be wrong. Another thing is to admit that you have probably not yet seen all sides of an issue yourself. And another idea is to ask others for their ideas and help.

As stated in chapter 9, the founder of Motorola, Paul Galvin, is reported to have developed the capacity to invite helpful ideas from his employees. In the course of running his business, Paul Galvin managed to convince his associates that he did not consider himself infallible. They soon learned that they could go to him and say, "Paul, your decision yesterday was wrong." If the new facts they supplied stood the test of his scrutiny, he would accept their analysis. Some recall his words, "Tell the fellows we're changing. My decision yesterday was wrong." He pursued good, clear thinking and did not stand on his position or office, because he was not too arrogant or proud to back down or accept other ideas. Results were what he was after. Paul Galvin often said, "Follow the right decisions regardless of when, or how, or by whom these decisions were arrived at." Here was a man who was particularly impatient with those who could not admit their own mistakes. This might sound like strange advice in our competitive world. What happens to people who act this way? It might surprise you. They are admired and they move ahead.

Douglas Danforth, former chairman and CEO of Westinghouse, once told me he did just that—admit his mistakes. His experience serves as a wonderful standard in humility. He said to me, "With the board of directors, when I make a mistake, I tell them I have made a mistake. They love it. And they are more supportive of me than if I had tried to hide it. I clearly think it's a much better policy. And, you sleep better—you really do!" So, go ahead, admit your mistakes. It makes you human—and a lot more believable.

Learn to Profit from Honest Criticism

"The most important criterion for any teacher is honesty," said Jean-Pierre Rampal, the great flutist. "It's necessary to say what you believe is true about the way a student plays. For some people," says Rampal, "this is a bitter pill to swallow."

One day a young American girl played for him. He stopped her after she had played only a few measures. Rampal tried to explain that she played the music badly; she needed to work harder. "My dear, the sound isn't good, the technique is faulty and what you played sounded bad," he told her.

With tears in her eyes, the flustered girl protested: "No one has ever spoken to me like that before." Her response carried the implication—how dare you!

Rampal told her that he didn't want to hurt her feelings but he wasn't about to lie to her. "What good would it be to say '*bravo, c'est magnifique!*' when the whole class can hear that you play badly?" By the time she dried her eyes, the girl had begun to understand that her teacher wanted to help. She resigned herself to honest criticism and to work harder. The maestro spoke only the truth to his students and if they wanted to learn, then hearing that truth was the price they'd have to pay.

Some people are only hurt by criticism; they are incapable of turning it into a source of help. They have such confidence in their skill, their wisdom, and their judgment, that it never occurs to them that they are fallible. We all know people like this. As long as others compliment them, they are pleased. But let someone dare criticize or even question whether there could be an improvement and they are offended. They regard as an enemy anyone who as much as intimates the slightest measure of disapproval or hints, however delicately, that they might do better. The person who resents and rejects criticisms cuts off the best means of growth and improvement. This person is no longer teachable. This person is incapable of benefiting from the opinions of others.

Pride. It is a powerful emotion that prevents us from knowing the truth about ourselves and it eliminates the possibility for any improvement. Apparently what happens is that when pride gets the better of us, we cannot bear to humble ourselves to standards, particularly those that we have not yet reached. We are unable to say, "I have failed. I am not as good as I think I am." Pride makes us want to think so highly of ourselves that any time we fail to achieve a high standard, we immediately disparage that standard or we assert that the measurement of our performance against that standard is faulty. So, there we are, trapped by our pride, unable to improve.

There are two ways to respond to factual information about oneself. One way is to see it as an offensive "put down." The other way is to see it as a source of help. Pride will determine how a person chooses between these two possibilities and whether the consequence will be either harmful or helpful.

I hesitate to tell this next story for fear it be mistaken as self-flattery. I hope it isn't that and will go ahead and tell it anyway, because I believe many people can relate to it and might profit from its simple message. When I was a Boy Scout I wanted to earn the pioneering merit badge. To earn that badge you had to either construct a bridge in the woods or build a model bridge. It was plainly evident to the merit badge counselor that I was far more interested in earning the pioneering merit badge than I was in the subject itself. And my model bridge reflected that fact. It was a flimsy, hastily pieced together bundle of sticks with little thought behind it. The super structure wasn't a super structure at all. It was just twigs tied together with string in an arch shape. The merit badge counselor wasn't impressed with it and he said so. He explained that before he'd pass me on the pioneering badge I'd have to learn quite a bit more about bridge construction—how superstructures work, how they hold up loads, that some members of the structure are under tension and others are under compression. He told me that I needed to understand how these forces had to cancel each other out at any point.

Like most youngsters facing a situation of failure, I was disappointed. For a short while I felt he was too harsh on me. I even thought about finding another merit badge counselor that would be more "reasonable." And, I wanted to forget about that merit badge altogether. Who needed it, anyway? Luckily these thoughts and feelings left me. My dad produced one of his college textbooks on structures and I read a section that explained how trusses work. It then became clear why my bridge model was woefully inadequate.

I resolved to try again. This time I'd apply the knowledge I had gained about trusses. My bridge would have a Warren truss, shaped in the form of an inverted "W." I carefully drew a full-size bridge truss plan on a large sheet of paper and cut small sections of wood in the correct lengths. Then I lashed them together as the Scout manual showed they ought to be tied. Now, I had a model bridge I was proud of. It had a properly designed truss. I confidently returned to the merit badge counselor several weeks later with my model bridge and he approved me for the pioneering merit badge.

After signing the merit badge form he told me then that he was a "tough old Scoutmaster from Pittsburgh" and that whenever he passed a Scout on a merit badge, that Scout knew the subject. He said, "I didn't know if you'd ever be back. I knew that if you didn't come back, you'd probably never learn about bridge construction. But if you did, as you have now, you'd have really learned something." Now the important thing to learn from this story is how we can move from the worst kind of failure to the finest kind of success. The answer lies in overcoming our pride. It lies in first humbling ourselves to time-honored standards that civilization has come to realize are worth having and worth respecting.

It is a kind of paradox when you think of it: to become great, one must first admit to his smallness and humble himself before high standards. But this is never easy, because pride is ever present and must first be conquered. Learn to conquer pride and improvement becomes possible.

All persons of depth and insight know that pride can keep them from knowing the truth about themselves. But pride's destructiveness runs deeper. It can even trick people into thinking their faults go unnoticed. Although they may have faint glimpses of these faults, their pride whispers in their ear that nobody else sees them. When this occurs a person remains permanently plagued by their limiting weaknesses. Because it declares "false" to the slightest criticisms one might receive from time to time, it chokes off any possibility for self-improvement.

Give Credit to Those Who Earned It

Pride can hold back otherwise able people from becoming effective leaders. This is because those who are infected with pride are intolerant. They regard others as being unworthy of dignity and respect. But with pride in check, practically anything is possible.

Harry B. Cunningham, the man credited with being the father of Kmart, was a person who had this special touch with people. His subordinates said that he was one of the most gracious men they ever had the pleasure of working for. There are people in business who are afraid to compliment their people. Harry Cunningham was just the opposite. He would compliment employees even when, perhaps, they didn't fully deserve it. And his employees would go out and break their necks to make sure they deserved it the next time he came around. He was that type of person: He built people up and they stretched to become the kinds of employees he projected them to be.

That's leadership. It's giving credit where credit is due. It's not trying to hog all the credit oneself. I once had lunch with Don Petersen, who was chairman of Ford Motor Company at the time. Don had recently been rated as America's most admired chief executive by *Fortune* but you'd never know it from talking to him. He was as easy to talk to as anyone I've ever met. Why should he be any other way? He certainly did not need to impress anyone, especially me. One of the things we chatted about during our visit was the nature of business reporting in the news media. Stories of CEOs in newspapers and business magazines have a tendency to personalize the achievements of the chief executive. "How does one prevent that sort of thing from going to his head?" I asked him. Don answered this way: "I do not dream up, design, develop, manufacture, assemble, and sell a product, all by myself! It is a team process that has been going on for some considerable time." Ford is a huge company, made up of tens of thousands of highly capable, dedicated people. An effective leader never forgets that.

Gertrude Boyle, chairman of Columbia Sportswear, called herself a seamstress and refused to take credit for the accomplishments of the growing firm she guided for 25 years. "The company owes its success to its employees," she said. "No one person does it on his own. Anyone who says they do is deceiving themselves."

A Service-Oriented Attitude Defeats Pride

When a person has a cause that captures his full loyalty and devotion and he has forgotten himself in its pursuit, he will discover that no job to that end is beneath him. The only important thing is that the work goes forward, productively. In this spirit, all the tasks that contribute toward its achievement will be carried out cheerfully. The dedicated, loyal person does not think of himself as so important that he can refuse to perform whatever menial work is needed. I see this trait in the lives of great leaders. The leader who serves his followers, that they might perform their work, is a great leader. And the one who denies himself the temptation of resting on his position as an excuse for not pitching in when he can give assistance often becomes an admired leader. We can also catch a glimpse of this excellent idea from the following anecdote about the United Parcel Service founder and former chairman, Jim Casey.

A small contingent of top UPS managers was staying at a motel once. This group, which included Jim Casey, worked round the clock preparing for hearings in an intrastate application for operative rights. One evening during their stay a group of the managers met in a large parlor. It was chilly and a little drafty. One of the men felt his throat grow scratchy and he worried out loud about getting a cold. He was concerned that a sore throat and a case of the sniffles could hurt his part of the presentation the next day. He inquired as to whether anyone had any cough drops, but no one did. Although he was not directly a part of the proceedings, Jim Casey was in the room at the time. Moments later he disappeared. After about an hour the chairman returned with several packages of cough drops. He had quietly slipped away and walked a mile along the main highway to the nearest store where he had bought the cough drops. It was Mr. Casey's attitude that if there were any way he might be able to help other than just sitting around, why shouldn't he do it? In Chairman Casey's words, "Any of us who can help the company get rights ought to do it. And, if cough drops help and I can get the cough drops, I ought to be the one."

The repeated act of serving shapes us into more than just productive workers. It leads us to become wonderful people, who truly care about others. George Schaefer, who ran Caterpillar Tractor, told me about the first boss he had at that company. It was when George was just starting out in their accounting department. The boss was a big Swede, who was the general auditor of the company, and he was tough and he was thorough—and some even thought he was mean, so gruff was his exterior. But, he was a man of high principles and a man with a heart as big as you could find. One example shows this.

Schaefer had been sent out to Caterpillar's California plant to work. He was called back to Peoria for a meeting in mid April. And, of course, it was already warm and sunny out in California. But when he arrived in Peoria a cold snap came sweeping down from the north. It got down to 25 degrees. When he walked into the office the next morning without a coat on, the general auditor asked: "George, Where's your coat?" George said that he didn't think to bring one; he thought the weather would be warmer. The kind-hearted Swede went home and brought one of his coats back for George to wear. It was only a small thing, but it shows something large—an attitude of helpfulness. Just imagine what young George felt about his boss because of it. It is a good example anyone would do well to emulate.

A great tragedy is always present when a person gives most of his efforts to what matters the least and gives least to what matters the most. Self-centeredness is boring. It is about as interesting and useful as last year's bird nest. A person who is more concerned with an important cause than he is with his sense of self-importance is free to act nobly and courageously and thus make possible what, otherwise, might never be accomplished.

Defeating Pride

Let's consider practical action steps you can take to defeat the destructive powers of pride.

1. Watch that you don't spend time admiring yourself and your accomplishments. Be too busy with working on a new challenge to have time for self-congratulatory thoughts.
2. Don't overrate yourself and don't take credit for giving yourself your talents and your love for doing what you like doing.
3. Admit your limitations. Ask for suggestions and ideas from others and listen to these.
4. Learn from criticism. Humble yourself before high standards of quality performance.
5. Give other people the credit that they deserve. Don't try to grab credit and rewards for yourself.
6. Become helpful, doing whatever needs doing to get the job done.

CHAPTER 15

Improve Your Ability to Perform

Keep your mind alive and growing

It is a law of life—a person is either, growing or stagnating, getting better or falling behind. What nature gives us in terms of talents and aptitude can either be used and improved or left to decay. It all depends on what we choose to do with ourselves. You can always tell which direction a person's abilities are growing by what that person does after completing a piece of work. Whether the work performed turned out to be a smashing success or a colossal failure, the person who is growing larger reveals this fact by finding lessons to be learned from the job just finished and by taking steps to improve.

Some people look upon work as being something that they do to things, by using information and manipulating objects. While they think and take actions, sometimes in cooperation with others, they view their work as being a process that flows from themselves to the object created or the work performed and it stops there. Other people view their work as involving something more, something basic to their own vitality. While they see work as being what they do to things, they also view it as an experience that can have a profound affect on themselves. They see work as an experience that shapes them as persons, and the possibilities for how they can be shaped are as endless as the possibilities for the kinds of work they might perform.

"This job taught me to be a better listener," said one woman. "I learned that if I didn't pay close attention to callers when they said their name, I wouldn't catch it, and then I'd create a bad impression when I had to ask them their name later on. Now I listen carefully when someone says their name. You know, this ability is very useful when it comes to everyday personal contacts." A man who had created a beautiful design and crafted it into a lovely work of art said, "This piece of work was fun to do; I loved the challenge. I now see things differently in terms of balance and mass than when I started the project. But as much as people admire it, I know of several flaws it has, mistakes I made. There are several things that I'd do differently were I to make another one." This is honesty in action.

The Desire to Improve Oneself

One distinguishing quality of an honest person is the habit of assessing their own performance. It takes a good bit of integrity after viewing a piece of work to say where it turned out poorly and where it turned out superbly. It takes even more honesty and imagination to say how that piece of work could be performed better. And it takes even more honesty and imagination still to improve oneself. Consider the following:

James received a poor annual evaluation from his boss because his performance declined significantly in an important area. He listened carefully to what the boss told him and resolved on the spot to remedy his deficiency. During the next several days James sat down and developed a plan to overcome his weakness. He set improvement targets, enrolled in a seminar that promised to sharpen deficient skills, and he created a list of habits that he believed would reinforce his application of better work habits.

Sheila had an excellent year. Her unit surpassed its goals and her boss couldn't be happier. But Sheila believes that now is not the time to allow complacency a chance to gain a foothold. She called a meeting with her unit to discuss their past year's performance, at which time they created a list of the reasons for their successful year. They also identified areas where they think can do better in the future.

The difference between the ordinary performer and extraordinary one, over time, is traceable to the will to improve and the habit of turning every experience into a valuable lesson. Extraordinary performers look at work as being something that has possibilities for changing them for the better. The stories of these two people—one trying to rise above a weakness and the other fresh off the heels of a spectacular success—make evident the value of saying "yes" to self-improvement opportunities.

All too frequently self-improvement opportunities are missed because other forces within one's character win out in the competition for expression, which invite stagnation and mental rigidity. The kinds and nature of these hideous, competing, inner forces are many. One of them is insecurity. To the insecure person, any hint, let alone any hard evidence, of a deficiency is seen as an unbearable sore, which must be avoided or met with hostile contempt and fiery denials. Painful news can also evoke counterattacks upon the bearer of bad news, so strongly stung is the insecure person's ego. Many poor performers remain mired in the clutches of mediocrity, because their insecurities prevent them from facing their deficiencies. Instead of making an honest assessment and having the fortitude to improve, they insist that either the evaluation was flawed or the evaluator is an enemy with an agenda to destroy them.

Success can also invite destructive forces that stop cold further self improvement. A materialistic person sees results as the only thing that matters. This person is blind to the deeper, spiritual joys derived from achievements. This limited perception brings on a tendency to ease up and coast a bit right after a success. If the world is entirely material in nature, as they see it, then only material results have meaning. It is understandable, therefore, why once they attain what they aspired to achieve, any further effort is unnecessary. It is also understandable why these people might not be able to weather failures in performances and have the motivation and drive necessary to gladly accept criticism.

Humans have a powerful weapon in the form of their capacity to love, and it is what they love that most determines their capacity and inclination to continually improve themselves. Here is how this capacity can be of help in the process of self-improvement. Suppose that my chief interests, my abiding concerns, were with something that gives me great pleasure, not from the records of successes and compliments that flow to me and flatter my ego and not from the material rewards obtained but from the simple act of doing of my work. If these conditions existed, then I would be living on a different level. Namely, I would be more alive to doing things than having things, more concerned with authenticity than with recognition, more driven to answer a summons from powers beyond my own than to please my own ego. If I were such a person, I would find a never-ending stream of delights and adventures as I pursued my calling. I would be so concerned with achieving authentic results for a cause that I cared for deeply that I would gladly humble myself and continue to learn so as to be able to serve my chosen calling better in the days ahead.

The Possibility of Mental Stagnation

Up until about the age of 25, people generally grow stronger and more able to perform physical work. After that, the aging process begins to take hold, and it begins to move us in a different direction. Our agility and strength begin to decline. We grow less able to do as much as we could before. This generalization applies to virtually every part of the human body except one, the mind. The brain can continue to increase its powers far into later life. It all depends on how it is used. Our mental powers and spiritual qualities can be perfected through constant use, and especially when they are challenged to work harder. But let the mind rest too long, remove all challenge and novel experience from it, and it will grow weak and flaccid. As with body muscles, the mind will waste away if not exercised regularly. Do the same things day after day, don't experience new challenges, remove the possibility of challenge, and limit what you read or see and the people you encounter. This is the perfect prescription for rigidity and narrowness of thought, a sure and quick route to obsolescence.

It has been said that one of life's great tragedies occurs when a person's mind and heart die out, while the rest of the body lives on. Over time, we've all seen it; many people lose their enthusiasm for living. They grow cynical about the future. Their mental alertness declines. Their zest for enjoying things good dwindles. Their inclination and ability to notice beauty and things meaningful and humorous grind to a halt. They become unable and unwilling to savor the moment. We are all vulnerable to these sad endings. Unwanted and unnoticed forces assault us daily, pushing us toward mental stagnation and its evil cousin, cynicism. These forces include: unthinking habit, fear of failure, doing just enough to get by, procrastination, over reliance on old solutions and methods, avoidance of opportunities and new endeavors because they seem too complex or difficult, unchanging routine void of new experience, and the attitude, "I already know enough to get by."

Self-Improvement

The surest way to prevent the tragedy of rigidity and mental decay is by keeping one's self mentally active with different and difficult challenges. Hearts and minds not exposed to novelty die prematurely. But through self-renewal—a process of regeneration to keep our minds alive and growing—we can avoid mental stagnation. There are practical things any one can do. These include: new experiences, hobbies, travel, new friends and acquaintances, continuing education, volunteering your time for worthy causes, serving others in your community, reading. The aim should always be in view and pursued deliberately and conscientiously: to avoid mental and emotional death. And the way to achieve that aim is through ongoing learning and new experiences. Doing this puts a person one step nearer a richer, fuller, more productive and more satisfying life.

When the prospect for self-improvement presents itself to a practical person, it's amazing what can happen. Here is an illustration of what I mean. Sanford McDonnell, who once ran McDonnell-Douglas, the aircraft maker, told me about his experience. I think his honesty in self-assessment sets a high standard of honesty and humility that everyone would do well to emulate. Sandy said that his experience arose as a result of his being active in the Boy Scouts with his son. He was tremendously impressed with the impacts that the Scout oath and laws were having on the young people. He recognized that the primary mission of scouting is to instill those values in young boys.

Being their Scout leader, Sandy spent time talking about the organization's oath and laws. Then one day, after telling Scouts to live up to the code, a question entered his thoughts: "What am I doing to live up to this oath and the Scout laws? They could just as well apply to me as to the Scouts." Self-examination followed and, like anyone else, he recognized that in many ways he was falling far short on some of these ideals himself. Then he got to thinking some more: "Here I am, head of McDonnell-Douglas, this giant aircraft manufacturer and defense contractor. We expect our employees to be ethical, but what does that really involve? We need a written code of ethics." This led him to assemble a small taskforce of top people. He told them, "Here are the Boy Scouts of America's Oath and Laws. Develop a code of ethics for our company, patterning it after the Scout oath and laws. I want you to cover every point in there." This they did. The McDonnell-Douglas Code of Ethics was based on the Boy Scout laws.

As we consider this story, several lessons stand out. Here was a person exposed to something in the realm of the ordinary and, seeing it with a fresh mind, honestly took it to heart. Self-examination, an indispensable ingredient to change and improvement, occurred and definite actions followed that bridged the divide between abstract idea and hard reality, vital betterment.

Expect Learning Opportunities to Come from Unexpected Places

Sandy McDonnell's experience demonstrates another powerful truth: Any time the human mind goes to work on one problem, it usually finds solutions to other problems that are linked to it. If, for example, we ask ourselves, "How can we become more productive?" and then use our creative powers to find answers, thoughts about product quality improvements are bound to crop up too. Author Tom Peters, of *In Search of Excellence* fame, shows repeatedly that productivity and quality are not mutually exclusive. Frequently, a solution to one of these aims leads to improvements in the other one as well.

This is what the people at NYNEX, the telephone company serving the northeast, discovered when employee teams sought to improve performance quality a number of years ago. In contradiction to the oft-spoken remark, "We can improve quality but it will cost a lot more," experience shows us the case is just the opposite. When teams from NYNEX went to work on a problem of finding ways to improve product quality and customer service, for example, their efforts produced a spillover effect. In reaching for solutions to improved quality, they unexpectedly found many ways to do the same things more economically too.

One never knows what might spark a change in a person. But we do know that humans are capable of remarkable change. It all depends on the experience and the person and whether they honestly examine what's happening. Self-reflection usually holds tremendous possibilities and usually for the good—particularly if it is done with an open mind. An important mark of honesty is the ability to remove one's blind spots, to see and value things previously not seen. It takes a big mind to tolerate a new perspective and an open heart to embrace a change.

A man named Richard Clarke told me of such a change in himself that he experienced. It had happened many years earlier when he was an attorney responsible for arguing a rate case before the California State Legislature on behalf of Pacific Gas and Electric. Richard Clarke was a smart and hard-working attorney who prided himself in always being fully prepared for hearings and court cases. A proposal came before the California legislature. It was for a utility rate schedule, called a "lifeline" concept, which would add a social dimension to rate-making. If the proposal passed, utility companies would be forced to charge standard rates for all customers, regardless of whether providing electricity to them cost the utility companies more than the customer's energy bills would total. If this legislation passed, PG&E would, therefore, lose money selling electricity to some customers at below their cost. That was the issue. Richard Clarke went to Sacramento to convince state legislators that the proposal was irrational. And he was prepared to show what would be the negative consequences. He had reams of empirical data and carefully crafted arguments. PG&E and all the other energy providers, he would argue, should not have to depart from cost-based rates. That would be irrational. The energy providers believed that utility rates should be based on the cost of serving particular customers.

On the morning of the hearing, Richard Clarke walked into the hearing room prepared with facts and figures and carefully reasoned arguments. But the people arguing for the other side, those who were supporting the proposal, had brought in busloads of senior citizens and members of the clergy. The hearings began. Clarke's mind was filled with facts and cleverly reasoned arguments and there, sitting in the hearing room, were senior citizens who had high energy bills to pay. His mind had one agenda but his heart felt something different. He suddenly became aware of another dimension. It was something beyond hard, cold calculations. The hearing room was packed with clergy, elderly gentlemen and lovely, little old ladies. He thought to himself, "One of them could be my grandmother." As the hearing went forward and he and his assistants presented their facts, these fine people just sat there, and they would grimace and grunt as he showed his charts and calculations and talked about the costs his company faced. These people didn't know about those things. They had a real need that demanded a practical solution, an answer that wouldn't break their pocketbooks. In the end, the legislators didn't buy his eloquent rhetoric. They responded to the feelings (and votes) of the elderly people sitting there.

But this experience turned out to be more to Richard Clarke than a lost case. It worked its effect on him. While he failed to convince legislators to vote against the proposal, he won a larger prize—the ability to see economic issues from an entirely different perspective. What happened that day changed him. He told me that the experience taught him something terribly important: to be more customer sensitive and understanding of the human dimension in markets and business. And these were critical character-building influences that added a very special dimension to a very bright man. What he learned must have made a difference. For, you see, in the years that followed Richard Clarke rose to become chairman and CEO of Pacific Gas and Electric, the country's largest utility company. And what was it, exactly, that he learned from his experience? "That," he told me, "more than any event that I can think of, really underscored to me the importance of dealing with needs and feelings, and that you can't rationally persuade or discount feelings and sensitivities. They are as much a part of the equation as the intellectual side is. And also, it just drove home the fact that as a company we have to be caring." The experience was an invitation to change. And by choosing to learn from it, he made himself into an effective leader.

Make On-going Learning a Regular Part of Your Work

Human nature, it would seem, is such that we are inclined to report on the things we've done well. We all like to feel that we're pretty good. This tendency, I think, is holding many people back from never fully realizing the potential improvements that their life's lessons could bring. It is also true that our desire for approval is oftentimes far stronger than our desire for improvement. Those who are wise enough to realize this make themselves strong enough to do something about it by asking themselves a profound question: "What do I prefer for myself—comfort or improvement?"

CIGNA, the insurance giant, has a process that has become a tradition. Any time senior management at corporate headquarters does a "post mortem" on decisions and major actions, they ask themselves, "What lessons did we learn from this?" It may be something that went wrong or it could be something that went very well. How it turned out isn't the issue. The important thing is, "What can be learned from the experience?" This is, indeed, an effective method for identifying ways to improve.

The next time you try something, it is a useful technique to conduct an after-the-fact audit of the experience to identify "Lessons Learned." Ask yourself, "What do we now know that we didn't know before, because of this experience?" Of course, one great value of this is to identify mistakes so they will not be repeated. But realize that there is the positive value to be gained, also.

Learn from What Others Have to Say

It's never easy to learn the truth about yourself. Of course, this can be rough—especially if one has a long pattern of rejecting all the little hints that have been coming their way over a long time. While it's hard to bear the painful sting of criticisms, wise and honest persons ask this question whenever they hear criticism of themselves: Can I tolerate the fruits of my shortcomings?

One of the most important questions anyone truly interested in self improvement can ask is, "From whom can we obtain reliable information about ourselves?" Friends are often quite tender and, hence, unwilling to provide painful information. They don't want to offend. And, having likes and dispositions that mesh well with ours, they are apt to be much like us and not likely to notice our faults. In truth they may tend to perceive more virtues in us than shortcomings.

An adversary, however, is more likely to serve as a fruitful monitor. Propelled by dislike, he is sure to ferret out our slightest slip-ups and defects and to make these known in such large and alarming ways that even we cannot miss them. A person who is willing to give due consideration to distasteful challenges; is, indeed, an open-minded individual. Nathan Ancell, the man who co-founded Ethan Allen Furniture, developed enormous respect for a man by the name of Bill Morrissey who worked for him but wasn't afraid to say what he thought. And Nathan listened to what Bill had to say, because Nathan was wise enough to know that truth can come from anyone.

Early in its history Ethan Allen acquired a small furniture factory where Bill worked. Despite the fact that he reported to Nathan Ancell, Morrissey wrote to him in longhand in four-, five-, and six-page letters, in which Bill questioned everything his boss, Nathan, was doing. Bill told his boss that he was worried the company was going to take advantage of his factory and take advantage of the people who worked there. He challenged Nathan strongly and questioned his moves.

Most people would have said that Bill Morrissey didn't know Nathan Ancell well enough to be so blunt and forceful, to challenge his decisions and actions as Bill did. And, Bill really didn't know whether his boss's motives were make-believe or whether they were genuine and honest. Still, Bill challenged Nathan like no employee would ever challenge a boss. He had guts. And he wasn't afraid. And by challenging his boss honestly and straightforwardly, Nathan's respect for Bill grew by leaps and bounds. Nathan Ancell must have valued Bill's letters, because he's kept all of them in his vault as a reminder of an honest man. They were that important to him.

Getting the level of honesty that Nathan got from Bill is particularly difficult—especially if one is in a powerful position. People won't tell those at the top about their shortcomings; they're scared to do that. So, what is a person on top supposed to do? Thomas J. Watson, Jr., former chief executive of IBM, understood the importance of hearing what others thought. He put this powerful idea into words when he explained, "I never hesitated to promote someone I didn't like. The comfortable assistant, the nice guy you like to go on fishing trips with, is a great pitfall. Instead I looked for those sharp, scratchy, harsh, almost unpleasant guys who see and tell you about things as they really are. If you can get enough of them around you and have the patience enough to hear them out, there is no limit to where you can go."

Be Curious: Look for Opportunities to Learn

Samuel Johnson, that great English scholar and philosopher (1709–1794), captured a vital truth when he said that curiosity is a characteristic of a vigorous intellect. Curiosity prods us to admit what we don't understand. And, it pushes us to overcome our ignorance with new knowledge.

This is exactly what Douglas Danforth, former chairman and CEO of Westinghouse, urged young men and women who worked in his organization do—become curious. "Have a curiosity about what's around you," he told them. "In the business world, if you start out in engineering, have a curiosity about marketing, about manufacturing, about finance. Don't let yourself stay just within your own envelope or your own discipline. Because people are very willing to share their knowledge and experience, the most flattering thing you can do is to ask them, 'Tell me a little about what you do in marketing. I don't understand anything about it. Would you mind having lunch with me, or if I stopped by after work, would you chat with me? Could I make a trip with you to call on a customer? I've never sold anything.'"

When he was a young man starting out in his career, this is what Danforth did, himself. Because he was curious, he asked questions, lots of questions. And he learned from the answers he received. And because of that, he grew. He began his career in manufacturing. But when he looked out upon his company, he saw a broad vista of learning opportunities. He wanted to know more about these other areas. Marketing and finance aroused his interest. And the more he learned, the more he saw there was to learn. Demonstrating a bit of curiosity served him well, and he moved from one job to another, all the way to the very top of his company.

It's impossible to be curious unless you are humble. Socrates opened many pair of eyes to what humility involves when he said, "I neither know nor think that I know." The important lesson to be grasped here is this: It is humility that allows people to recognize their ignorance. Once humility is reached, curiosity can arise and lead to improvement.

The capacity to wonder is at the heart of curiosity. Imagine a small child on a summer's day, lying on the ground watching ants scurrying about, toting what appear to be tremendous loads in comparison to their tiny bodies. Curiosity involves looking at things and asking oneself questions: "What makes it work? How does it happen?" But these are only a start.

The curious person is continually looking up the spellings and definitions of new words encountered. Curious minds are no stranger to encyclopedias and reference books. People who are curious thirst for ideas and information. And they do this for no other reason than they want to know more. They admit that they have no idea where cloves come from. So, they look that up. They hear about cinnabar and ask themselves what that is. And they look that up. They consult maps to locate where places are that they have heard mentioned in the news but don't know about, places like Kuala Lumpur. And they stop to observe things (we are not talking about people watching at bars and airports) and try to figure out how they work or can be fixed.

Look for Weaknesses, where Improvement Is Most Needed

It is easy to think you have it made whenever you have a record of success. But the pursuit of perfection says "no" to the easy and "yes" to great challenges that you can set before yourself to achieve. Here is an outstanding illustration of what I mean. Tim Boyle, CEO of Columbia Sportswear in Portland, Oregon, probes customers' minds. He is keenly interested in knowing what they like and dislike about the rugged outerwear his company makes, and he's eager to modify what they do not like. Several times each year, Tim invites buyers from stores around the country to accompany him to the great outdoors. They go to rugged spots like Montana where his guests hunt or fish. Tim calls these outings "cast-and-blast" outdoor adventures, and they are fun. But there are lessons to be learned too. These adventure outings are Tim's laboratory for testing Columbia's products.

From his cast-and-blast outings Tim Boyle returns with fresh ideas for new products or modifications to existing ones. The secret to his success lies in his ability to listen. From doing this he has also developed a keen eye for sensing something that isn't quite right. On a recent adventure Tim supplied his guests with fishing vests. They mentioned they'd like it if the pockets were larger to hold their fly boxes. He fixed that, redesigning slightly larger pockets. On a duck hunting trip Tim noticed that his Columbia hunting jackets were inadequate— all his guests shivered from the cold. There was a strong wind and everyone got chilled on the back of the neck. He improvised improvements on the spot by removing a collar from another Columbia jacket and wedging it into the hunting jacket.

Look at Setbacks as Opportunities to Improve

Difficulties can become growth stimulators, provided you see them as invitations to improve. The Russians have a proverb: "The hammer shatters glass but forges steel." People who are like steel can accept the setbacks life hurls their way and be changed for the better because of them. This seems to be a common trait of successful men and women. The great Russian composer Igor Stravinsky had this remarkable quality. Stravinsky revolutionized the music of his time. As early as 1913, Claude Debussy was praising him for having "enlarged the boundaries of the permissible" in music. And American composer Aaron Copland said Stravinsky's work had influenced three generations of American composers. Later, Copland revised his estimate to four generations and added European composers as well.

Stravinsky's parents sent him to the University of St. Petersburg to study law but his real passion was music. One of his classmates there was a son of composer Rimsky-Korsakov. In 1902, Stravinsky visited the great man, gave him some of his piano pieces for criticism, and asked if he could become his pupil. Rimsky-Korsakov studied them and told the 20-year-old Stravinsky that he'd need more technical preparation before he could accept him as a student. Shattered by this at first, Stravinsky decided to take it as encouragement. He went to work, as Rimsky-Korsakov said he ought, and a year later, after serious study, he applied to the master again and this time he was accepted. It was under Rimsky-Korsakov's supervision that Stravinsky composed his first orchestral works—a symphony, a suite (Le Faune et la Bergére), the *Scherzo Fantastique*.

We Can Shape Ourselves

A remarkable quality of human beings is their capacity to become persons largely of their own making. We are revisable documents, so to speak. What nature gives us and what our environment does to us are not the only variables in determining who we are and what we become. We can have a hand in the process of finishing ourselves. Think of it—we have the power to shape ourselves.

The implications of this fact are profound. To those who hold high ideals and want to do significant things with their lives, it means exciting and challenging opportunities and adventures are possible. You can live a big life, one that counts for something large by thinking big, by choosing to improve instead of allowing your abilities to stagnate, and by actively shaping yourself. The trick lies in giving your finest efforts to the few things that really matter. This involves keeping your mind alive, your self improving.

Let's summarize some of the things you can do to shape yourself into the kind of person you would like to become.

1. Try to learn something from everything you do. The ideal is ongoing self-improvement.

2. Realize that the feeling of "I must be perfect" can keep you from trying something new and from being honest with yourself as to how well you performed.

3. Be dead honest about your performance and your effectiveness. Let your mistakes become your teachers; put them to work and learn from them.

4. Let other people help you improve by giving hospitable thought to their comments and criticisms. Be open to new ways and different ideas.

5. Be curious about how things work, why things happen as they do. Let your curiosity take you into new, untried avenues.

6. Keep your mind alive. Get out of the comfortable habit of gliding along the groove of unthinking habit.

Additional Reading

Absolute Honesty: Building a Corporate Culture That Values Straight Talk and Rewards Integrity, Larry Johnson and Bob Phillips, AMACOM, 2003.

The Age of Moguls, Stewart Holbrook, Doubleday, 1954.

Authentic Happiness: Using the New Positive Psychology to Realize Your Potential for Lasting Fulfillment, Martin Seligman, Free Press, 2005.

The Behavior-Based Safety Process: Managing Involvement for an Injury-Free Culture, Thomas R. Krause, John Wiley & Sons, 1996.

Be My Guest, Conrad Hilton, Prentice-Hall, 1957.

The Ben Franklin Factor: Selling One to One, *James C. Hames, Morrow, 1992.*

Business as a Calling, Michael Novak, Free Press, 1996.

Callings: Finding and Following an Authentic Life, Gregg Michael Lovejoy, Three Rivers Press, 1998.

The CEO and the Monk, Robert B. Catell and Kenny Moore (with Glenn Rifkin) John Wiley & Sons, 2004.

"The Chairman of the Board Looks Back," Katrina Brooker, *Fortune*, May 14, 2001.

Do What You Love, The Money Will Follow: Discovering Your Right Livelihood, Marsha Sinetar, Dell, 1998.

"Fact and Comment," Malcolm S. Forbes, *Forbes Magazine*, July 13, 1987, pp. 33–34.

The Founder's Touch, Harry Mark Petrakis, McGraw-Hill, 1965.

From the Ninth Decade, J. C. Penney, Nelson, 1960.

From Worst to First: The Scenes of Continental's Remarkable Comeback, Gordon Buthane (with Scott Haler), John Wiley & Sons, 1998.

Grinding It Out: The Making of McDonald's, Robert C. Anderson, St. Martins Press, 1990.

Happiness: Lessons from a New Science, Richard Layard, Penguin Books, 2005.

Happiness Is a Choice, Barry Neil Kaufman, Ballantine Books, 1994.

"How Don Sheelen Made a Mess that Regina Couldn't Clean up," *Business Week*, February 12, 1990, p. 46.

The Integrity Advantage: How Taking the High Road Creates a Competitive Advantage, Adrian Gostick, Dana Telford, Mitt Romney, Gibbs Smith Publishers, 2003.

J. E. Casey, Our Partnership Legacy, United Parcel Service, 1985.

K-mart: Striving for a Comeback (Case Study) in *Crafting and Executing Strategy*, Arthur A. Thompson, Jr., A. J. Strickland, and John E. Gamble, McGraw-Hill-Irwin, 2005.

The Kroger Story: A Century of Innovation, George Laycock, Kroger Co., 1983.

Levi's, Ed Cray, Houghton-Mifflin, 1978.

Listening to Your Inner Voice: Discover the Truth Within You and Let It Guide Your Way, Douglas Block, Hazelden Publishing and Educational Services, 1991.

Main Street Merchant, Norman Beasley, Whittlesey House, 1948.

Milton Hershey, Builder, Joseph R. Snavely, Hershey, PA, 1935.

Moral Courage, Rushworth M. Kidder, William Morrow, 2005.

Portrait of an Artist: A Biography of Georgia O'Keefe, Laurie Lisle, University of New Mexico Press, 1986.

The Power of Boldness: Ten Master Builders of American Industry Tell Their Success Stories, Elkan Blout, et al., National Academies Press, 1996.

Radical Honesty: How to Transform Your Life by Telling the Truth, Bob Blanton, Dell, 1996.

The Resilience Factor: 7 Essential Skills for Overcoming Life's Inevitable Obstacles, Andrew Shatte and Karen Reivich, Broadway Books, 2002.

Safety Management: A Human Approach, 3rd ed., Dan Petersen, American Society of Safety Engineers, 2001.

The Servant: Simple Stories About the Essence of Leadership, James C. Hunter, Crown Business, 1998.

The Serving Leader, Ken Jennings and John Stahl-West, Barrett-Kohler, 2004.

The Survivor Personality, Al Siebert, Perigee Books, 1996.

The Transparent Leader: How to Build a Great Company Through Straight Talk, Openness &Accountability, Herb Baum and Tammy Kling, HarperBusiness, 2004.

Trust: The One Thing that Makes or Breaks a Leader, Les T. Csorba, Thomas Nelson, 2004.

The Turning Point: Pivotal Moments in the Lives of American Celebrities, Glenn Plaskin, Carol Publishing, 1992.

Unaccountable Accounting: Games Accountants Play, Abraham J. Briloff, Harpercollins, 1972.

"What Led Beech-Nut Down the Road to Disgrace?," Business Week, February 22, 1988, p. 124.

Why Courage Matters: The Way to a Braver Life, John McCain and Mark Salter, Random House, 2004.

The Writings of Benjamin Franklin, Smyth, Albert Henry, ed., Macmillan, 1907.

Index

About the Author

CHARLES E. WATSON is Professor of Management at Miami University in Ohio. He is the author of six books, including *What Smart People Do When Dumb Things Happen at Work* (Career Press, 1999) and *Managing with Integrity* (Praeger, 1991).